M000240222

127 Best Practices
For Accounts Payable

Mary S. Schaeffer, AP Now

Copyright © 2020 Mary S. Schaeffer All rights reserved.

Published by CRYSTALLUS, Inc.

No part of this publication may be reproduced, copied, stored in a retrieval system or transmitted in any form or by any means, electronic, mechanical, photocopying, recording, scanning or otherwise excepted as permitted by the US Copyright Act of 1976 without either prior written permission of the publisher or author.

Limit of Liability/Disclaimer of Warranty: The publisher and author have used their best efforts in preparing this book but make no representations or warranties with respect to the accuracy or completeness of the contents of this book and specifically disclaim any implied warranties of merchantability or fitness for a particular purpose. No warranty may be created or extended by sales representatives or written sales materials. The information contained herein may not be suitable for your situation. You should consult with a professional where appropriate. Neither the publisher nor author shall be liable for any loss of profit or any other commercial damages, including but not limited to special, incidental, consequential or other damages.

Parts of this book have been extracted from 101 Best Practices for Accounts Payable, the Accounts Payable Now & Tomorrow monthly newsletter and various talks given by Mary Schaeffer.

Bulk purchases can be arranged by contacting the author.

ISBN-13: 978-1-7351000-2-9

for

Ron Schacht

gone but not forgotten

CONTENTS

- Best Practice Policy
- Remote Working in Accounts Payable
- Policy and Procedures Manual
- Staff Training
- Dealing with Change and the Adoption of New Technology
- Soliciting Process Improvement Recommendations
- Payment Audits

- Who Has Access
- Master Vendor File Set-up
- Improve Upfront Vendor Validations for Twenty-first Century Issues
- Using Naming Conventions
- Contact Information in the Master Vendor File
- Making Changes to the Master Vendor File
- Master Vendor File Cleanup
- Self-service Master Vendor Files
- Checking for Employees as a Phony Vendors

- Receipt of Invoices
- Format for Receipt of Invoices
- Invoice Handling: Approvals
- Invoice Data Requirements
- Verifying Invoice Data

- Backup for Rush Checks/Payments

- Appropriate Segregation of Duties
- Appropriate System access
- Policy when Employees Leave
- Eliminating Weak Control Practices
- Staff Training
- ERP Access when There is a Change
- Who Should Receive Bank Statements

- Separate Computer for Online Banking
- Wire Transfer Information Requests
- Information on Internet for Vendors
- Mandatory Vacation Policy
- Job Rotation Policy
- Handling of Change of Bank Account Requests
- Rush Wire Transfer Requests from High Level Executives
- Requests for Sensitive Employee Information from High-Level Executives
- Educating Everyone in the Organization about New Frauds
- Quick Analysis: The 30-Second Smell Test
- Sharing Information on the Company Website

- Use of Positive Pay
- Pre-printed Check Stock Controls
- Check Stock Storage
- Other Check Fraud Prevention Practices

- Formal Policy
- Expense Report Form
- Verifying Data
- Handling Receipts
- Detailed Meal Receipts
- Use of a Personal Card
- Recovering Refunds on Personal Cards
- Reimbursements for Working from Home Expenses

- Cash Advances
- Unused Tickets
- Departing Employees
- Making Travel Reservations
- Reimbursing Employees
- Reporting of Use of Disruptive Services

- A Form W-9 Requirement Policy
- Collecting and Tracking W-9 and W-8 Policy
- Using IRS TIN Matching Properly
- Double Check 1099 Accuracy before Issuing or Reporting to IRS
- When to Request a New Form W-9
- The New Form 1099-NEC

- Reporting and Remitting Unclaimed Property
- Performing Due Diligence for Unclaimed Property
- Using Social Media to Track Rightful Owners of Unclaimed Property

LIST OF SKETCHES

ACKNOWLEDGMENTS

This book is the result of numerous conversations with many, many professionals who work in or manage the accounts payable function. A big thank you to all who graciously share their experiences—good, bad and bizarre. Some of their funny stories ended up as the sketches in this book.

And speaking of sketches, a big round of applause for Walter Moore, who managed to turn my ramblings into the wonderful drawings that grace this book. I hope they make you smile. I know I had a good chuckle or two.

I would be remiss if I did not mention Lynn Larson, who was a huge help in getting this project completed in record time—even my desire for speed did not match precisely with her penchant for attention to detail. And last, but definitely not least, my husband Hal, who is, as always, supportive of my endeavors, no matter how bizarre.

[*This first drawing is Walter's interpretation of one of my first Zoom meetings. I had shared with him that, demonstrating my lack of technical abilities, I had managed to project myself reversed. As I logged in, I could see my colleagues on the other end of the call, laughing hysterically as my head bobbed around upside down. Walter kindly turned the tables in the drawing.*]

INTRODUCTION

This book was written during the COVID-19 crisis. Things not only changed overnight, but for a while, it was quite grim. Accounts payable departments in many, many organizations took their work home and to the surprise of many, it worked. The country flirted with recession and unemployment skyrocketed. At this point it is too early to tell whether that will be long lasting or not. (Fingers crossed for not).

If we thought the accounts payable function had changed before COVID, the changes coming after it were amazing, most in a good way. Of course, skyrocketing fraud means a further tightening of fraud protection regimens.

In the last few years we've also seen a blurring of the lines between what we used personally and what is appropriate for business. Sites such as LinkedIn and Facebook (yes, Facebook) are mostly thought of in the realm of personal business. But savvy professionals have found ways to use both to run a more efficient accounts payable function. Today, most job listings for professionals are listed on LinkedIn, although that is not the only way LinkedIn can be used to run a more efficient accounts payable function. You'll have to read the book to get the details on its use as well as that of Facebook in the accounts payable arena.

The book analyzes 127 processes within the accounts payable function. This is up from 101 the last time I addressed the issue of best practices in a book. It incorporates the use of some disruptive services we now take for granted, new fraud protection protocols to address new frauds, and of course new best practices needed to address issues highlighted by the working from home phenomenon.

Just before the crisis erupted, less than one-quarter of all companies allowed their accounts payable staff to work remotely one or two days a week. It was viewed as a perk. That is changing. As we see companies realizing that their accounting staffs are just as productive, if not more so, when working remotely, combined with the financial benefits of the practice, remote working is no longer considered a luxury.

Each of the issues is explained and a best practice identified. More than occasionally, the best practice has several components so the explanations make take a few paragraphs. Recognizing that for a variety of reasons, an organization might not choose to or be able to utilize the preferred practice, the applicable second choice, the almost best practice is pinpointed. In some cases, there are none. There is only one right way to handle the particular issue.

Before honing in and identifying all the worst practices associated with a particular issue, we hone in on special pointers to help the accounts payable professional responsible for the issue. These are items that might not be obvious at first glance. The pointers also include some caveats and/or problems some might run into.

The work starts with a look at the accounts payable function and recommended practices to use when managing the function. For the first time, we've included a recommendation regarding remote working in accounts payable. It then moves on to what I believe should be the first step in the procure-to-pay practice, the master vendor file.

Since we're talking about a best practice world, we can assume the vendor will be set up in the master vendor file before the first purchase order is written, although that happens in only a minority of the cases. We've added some new best practices in this area, to help combat some of the newer frauds as well as to help organizations stay regulatorily compliant.

After the master vendor file, the book has two chapters on invoice processing and invoice problems, for alas there are many. Thanks again, to the recent crisis, there are some new recommended best practices regarding how companies receive invoices.

The book then looks at the end of the procure-to-pay process, the payment side. This includes chapters on paying by check, electronic payments and p-cards. It also examines several practices related to establishing an overall payment strategy, which every organization should do. There have been some innovations in the ACH world that have found their way into accounts payable best practices.

At that point, the book veers into a look at some of the background issues related to the accounts payable function. Despite the fact that they are not the ones that come immediately to mind when accounts payable is mentioned, handling them properly can mean operating a leading-edge best practice operation while ignoring them can lead to duplicate payments, fraud, IRS problems and other unpleasant outcomes.

The book has one chapter on the policy and procedures manual, an often-overlooked issue. It then delves into the operational aspects of accounts payable, a look at reducing duplicate payments and establishing strong internal controls. It should be noted that we expect many organizations will need to update their manuals after making some of the other changes recommended in this book. So, although you might be tempted, please don't skip this chapter.

Although we could have devoted a whole book to fraud, this was not the place for that and two chapters focus in on best practices that will help any organization prevent and detect fraud. I'd like to be able to report that there are no changes made in this area, but you'd know I was not being truthful. We've added a number of best practices we hope you are using because there have been several new types of cyber fraud focused directly on your accounts payable operations. You'll need these to ensure you are protected.

Equally voluminous could have been the space devoted to travel and entertainment practices, but again, they were relegated to two chapters delving into the policy and the thorny issues around expense reimbursements. We've also included the issue of reimbursing for remote working expenses and dealing with refunds for cancelled events, two issues that have become hot topics in the last few months.

No book on best practices would be complete without an examination of regulatory issues. So, we investigate best practices related to Information Reporting, 1099s, Unclaimed Property, Sales and Use Tax reporting and remitting, OFAC checking, and FCPA compliance. We've got some new practices here to help you improve your information reporting.

One of the areas that has experienced the most change is the way we use technology in accounts payable. The chapter on this issue delves into invoice automation, electronic invoicing, use of mobile devices (Smartphones and tablets) and establishing an overall technology strategy for the accounts payable function. And because so many people have been and/or will start working remotely, we've got some suggestions on dealing with technology.

Just because we rely on technology does not mean that communicating with vendors is still not critical. It is and we discuss several ways to disseminate information to them. And finally, we close with a look at cash flow issues. Accounts payable no longer operates as its own little silo. It is an integral part of the accounting and finance chain and as such, its impact on cash flow is discussed.

It's a whole new playing field and to be successful all organizations need to employ as many best practices as possible; for by their very nature best practices incorporate strong internal controls. What follows is a look at 127 accounts payable tasks and the best practices associated with each.

The Challenges of Working Remotely

Chapter 1: Managing the AP Function

When it comes to running an efficient accounts payable function, policies and procedures need to be set at the top, with the staff following directives and policies set by management. In this chapter, we will discuss:

- Best Practice Policy
- Policy and Procedures Manual
- Staff Training
- Soliciting Process Improvement Recommendations
- Payment Audits

The Issue: Best Practice Policy

Best practices are no longer set in stone. What worked yesterday may not work today or tomorrow. What's more, there have been a few instances where worst practices have turned into best practices. Automation, increased regulatory pressures and a relentless push for efficiency across the corporate spectrum have taken their toll. It is no longer possible to establish best practices and set the accounts payable wheels in motion and then forget about the process. Those days are gone.

Best Practice: Regularly review the practices used in your accounts payable function. Keep up-to-date on the latest changes. As you note where process improvements could be made, update your procedures and train everyone affected by the change. What's more, if you note a series of mistakes that require a process change in order to eliminate that error, make that improvement immediately. Once you've made the change, reflect it in your accounts payable policy and procedures manual and make sure everyone on staff is trained in the new methodology.

Almost Best Practice: Some organizations find it difficult to implement the type of continuous improvement cycle described above. For these firms, a once a year review and overhaul is the next best bet. Of course, this should be followed by an updating of the policy and procedures manual and retraining of the staff, should any changes be made. It is also possible that you'll do the annual review and from time to time, no changes will be required. However, don't count on that and skip the annual review. For if you skip it for a few years in a row, you are apt to find your processes are woefully out-of-date.

Special Pointers for Accounts Payable: It is imperative that any time you make a change to your practices, be it once a year or on an ongoing basis, everyone on staff is trained and all start using the new process at the exact same point. For if one does it one way and a second processor a different way, the odds of introducing errors and duplicate payments skyrocket.

Worst Practice: Not regularly reviewing and updating your practices to reflect current thinking related to best practices. For if there is no regular review, and you stick with the practices used in the past, before you know it your accounts payable function will be woefully out of date. This may mean missing a regulatory compliance issue that could get your company into hot water with the states or the Feds or duplicate payments, or increased likelihood of fraud.

The Issue: Remote Working in Accounts Payable

The issue of accounts payable professionals working remotely was as little as a few years ago considered a taboo issue in most organizations. It was rarely done. The temperature on this matter started to thaw a little bit a few years ago.

At the end of 2018, AP Now surveyed its readers and found that one-third of the respondents had a program that permitted employees in accounts payable to work remotely at least part of the time. While only a very few organizations had folks, who worked remotely 100% of the time, the remainder of the group had programs allowing people to work from home one or two days a week or in cases of emergency.

I had a preconceived notion on what the primary benefit would be and I was 100% wrong. We thought were the primary benefits coverage in bad weather and a slightly higher morale. Three times as many organizations focused on the higher morale. Perhaps the biggest surprise was the number of survey respondents who wrote in that they had experienced higher productivity once they started allowing remote workers.

Here are some of the other benefits reported:

They also spelled out other benefits including:

- The ability to keep qualified workers who were moving

- People working longer hours because they weren't wasting time commuting

- Employees who valued the flexibility remote working offers

- Allows for lower coverage during holiday periods

- Allows employees to work on days they would have previously had to take off thus reducing the strain on others who are in the office and would have to cover for them

- Less chit-chat

- Less space needed, saving organization on costly rents

- Traffic has gotten terrible in certain cities (Atlanta, Seattle and

Portland OR were mentioned several times.)

- Elevates employees to a higher sense of conscientiousness

- Very motivated employees

- Increased engagement

- Employees are more willing to work extra hours since they don't have commute time

- Turnover is almost non-existent

And then we had the coronavirus pandemic and issues like quarantine, self-quarantine and the cancelation of all sorts of events. Plus, many companies started to allow employees who were concerned or thought they might have been exposed to work remotely.

During the pandemic, AP Now regularly polled its readers about issues related to the new situation. Many, but definitely not all, were liking the new working environment. At the very beginning, virtually none of those working remotely thought their companies were likely to allow the practice to continue once the crisis ended. By the end, 38% expected their organizations to allow partial or complete working from home for the accounts payable staff.

Although the coronavirus outbreak is a contributor to the changing best practice in this matter, it is not the only reason. We've been heading this way for a long time, now that we have the technology that makes it possible and practical at little or no cost.

Best Practice: I'm sure you can see where this is going. At some point, there will be another crisis, possibly of even greater magnitude. Every organization should have a policy that requires each staffer to work from home at least one day per week. The purpose of this is so that should it become necessary to work remotely for longer periods; the infrastructure is in place to accommodate the process.

Additionally, the staff will be prepared to operate and the technology will be in place. One survey found that 15% of companies were going to invest in technology for their employees working remotely when the crisis ends. Only time will tell whether that actually happens.

Almost Best Practice: Every organization should have a policy that requires each staffer to work from home at least one day per month. The reasoning is as above. However, it is probably not as effective as once a week.

Special Pointer for Accounts Payable: While many professionals love to be able to work from home one or two days a week, there is a smaller group who do not want to do so. They may not have the space; they may live alone and look forward to the social aspects of going into a workplace or have another reason. However, the coronavirus crisis clearly demonstrated that every organization needs to be prepared.

Worst Practice: Doing nothing; not preparing operations for another crisis.

The Issue: Policy and Procedures Manual

The accounts payable policy and procedures manual should be the core document for the accounts payable department. It should document in detail the processes used within the department. Some refer to it as the bible for accounts payable. Having an updated accurate policy and procedures manual can come in handy if you are subject to an information reporting audit, a sales tax audit or an unclaimed property audit.

By being able to show documentation that demonstrates your good intent when it comes to these regulatory issues, you may be able to have fines or penalties abated. However, if the manual documents procedures that are not consistent with the law, the manual will not help you. A simple example might be if your policy and procedures manual shows that you routinely write un-cashed checks off to miscellaneous income instead of reporting and remitting them to the states. In this case your documentation would not show good intent and would not help you.

Best Practice: Any time you make a change in your processes, the manual should be immediately updated. Copies of the updated manual should be shared with all who are affected by the change or might need to know about it. Since these manuals are no longer printed but are usually a Word document saved as a PDF file, it is relatively easy to update and share – and there is no cost associated with printing new manuals. If no change has been made within the last 12 months, a quick annual review is a good idea.

Don't forget to update it once you update your processes for new best practices you implement post-COVID.

Almost Best Practice: If it is not possible to continually update the manual, save all changes for an annual review and update. Then, all recommended changes that came to light within the last year can be incorporated in one big update.

Special Pointers for Accounts Payable: The manual should not be a static document, but rather one that is used on a regular basis. Updated copies should be given to the existing staff to be used as a reference guide. This is particularly important if your accounts payable staff handles certain functions once or twice a year and may forget the details in the interim. They can turn to the manual instead of bothering the manager for the information they need. In fact, the staff should be encouraged to use the manual and only come to the manager if they can't find the answer in the manual.

Worst Practice: As you might expect, the worst practice regarding the accounts payable policy and procedures manual is creating a manual and then putting it on the shelf, never updating it or using it as a reference guide. This is a complete waste of time and effort. From time to time I am asked by those without a current manual, if they can buy one or simply download one off the Internet. While each of these approaches is possible, they won't give you a manual that reflects your current operations. They will require extensive review and editing. If you take someone else's manual, you get someone else's policies and procedures, which probably don't reflect what is going on in your shop.

The Issue: Staff Training

Keeping the staff up-to-date on changing best practices, changing regulatory requirements and new technology affecting accounts payable is not an easy task. This is on top of training the staff on the particulars of their day-to-day assignment. Unfortunately, due to the recent harsh recession, many organizations have cut training budgets to the bone. This has resulted in training falling to the already over-worked manager and has often just been skipped completely, with the idea that the organization will include training in next year's budget, or perhaps the following year. Given the pace of change in the business world, no organization can afford to skimp on training. But, that's exactly what has happened.

Best Practice: Budget for ongoing training for every single member of the staff. If this is not possible, take the do-it-yourself approach. Assign each staff member a topic for which they are to become the resident subject matter expert. Make them responsible for periodic updates at staff meetings. Even if it is not possible to send the entire team for training, if one person goes, they should be charged with updating their colleagues when they return from the event.

Almost Best Practice: Whether the organization has a budget for training or not, there are many low-cost or no-cost opportunities. Many vendors offer free webinars with a demonstration of their product at the end. Some complain about these product demos but I think they are missing the big picture. First, the product demo comes at the end, so if it is an online event, you can simply log out. But a better approach is to stay and listen to the product demo. This is a great way to learn what's on the market without having to deal with an aggressive salesperson in your office. You can devote as much or as little time to these presentations without worry about offending the salesperson. Don't overlook free electronic news alerts, from vendors and professional associations. One example is offered by the author's organization, AP Now.

Special Pointers for Accounts Payable: Attend as many of the vendor webinars described above so you will be conversant about new products on the market. You'll begin to see which ones would work best for your organization and which ones have features that your organization is not likely to use. One last point for accounts payable: If you see an event or a subscription that you think would benefit your organization if you were to attend, prepare a proposal for your boss. List the benefits for the company – not for you. You can get these by reviewing the list of topics and sessions to be covered at the event.

Worst Practice: Doing nothing because you either don't have budget or don't think management would approve the expenditure for training. There's a lot you can do on your own to keep up so there's no reason not to. And finally, if you ask to attend a particular function or event, the worst that can happen is your manager will say No. Then you are in exactly the same position as if you didn't ask. And, you may be pleasantly surprised.

The Issue: Dealing with Change and the Adoption of New Technology

Sometimes even the smartest, most motivated staffers seem to drag their feet when a new technology is introduced. This can be disheartening for those running the accounts payable function for often times, the decision has been made, the technology purchased and there is no turning back. Yet, the skeptics and naysayers will continue to dig in their heels resisting the change. This adds to the workload of the already overworked manager. What's going on and more importantly, what can you do to get them on board because, let's face it, if the decision has been made and the money spent, the new technology will be here to stay.

Best Practice: Don't ignore the situation. It will only get worse, aggravate management and impact the productivity of the group negatively. Here are a few steps you can take to ensure a successful launch of the new technology in your accounts payable function.

Step 1: Keep everyone in the loop. As soon as it becomes apparent that new technology will be used, start talking about it with the staff. Don't let them hear rumors from other departments or groups. They will always be exaggerated and make the situation worse. This can be an opportunity to build trust and team spirit. Update them on a regular basis on what's going on and especially if there have been successes in other departments.

Step 2: Address their fears. Ignoring the issue, hoping it will go away, is naïve. The fears won't disappear miraculously and the longer a staffer has to ponder over it and worry, the bigger the fear will become. So, rip the bandage off and address it right from the start. Be honest, even if the truth isn't pretty.

Step 3: Don't forget the WIIFT (what's in it for them) factor. This means pointing out the benefits of the new technology, not for the company, but for the end users, especially the staff concerned about losing their jobs. Maybe it means less keying of data and more time to do more value-add tasks. Or maybe it will mean the end of mandatory overtime. Focus on the benefits for them, not the company, when discussing it with the staff.

Step 4: If you are having a phased in approach, start with your early adopters and influencers. Get them onboard first and let them be your missionaries or evangelists singing the praises of the new technology. This means that the first few folks brought onboard might not be your most senior people but rather those that are likely to embrace the change. This may not sit well with your supervisors, especially if they are part of the group resisting the change. Plan on having a chat with them about this.

Step 5: Realize that the training is not likely to be a one-size fits all. Some of your staff will grasp the new technology right away and others will need additional time and effort. Customize the training to meet the individual needs of each staff person. You might have to run a more basic session for those who are not conversant with technology in general and a shorter, quicker session for the tech-savvy of your group. The important issue here is to make sure the training fits the needs of the individuals.

Step 6: Try taking a carrot approach to getting everyone to use the new technology. You can encourage usage by rewarding employees in ways that might be meaningful to them. For some it might simply be the opportunity to learn something new. But not everyone will fall into that group. Others might want something more material. This might mean time off, less overtime, a staff luncheon or something that they select.

Step 7: As much as possible, make the training and adoption entertaining. Injecting a little fun into the process will make people forget that they want to object. Of course, the fun aspects relate more to the training than the actual job, itself. How can you do that? For starters, try to introduce some aspects of gamification into the training. No one is expecting to play games and have fun when they go for training. So, incorporating game playing will be a surprise, and hopefully a nice one.

Almost Best Practice: One other approach is to set up a competition between different staff members. Or perhaps divide the group into a few small teams and let them compete. This will have the added benefit of having other team members encourage each other, rather than the manager being the bad guy who is insisting they make the change.

When all else fails, you'll need to take a harsher stance. At some point, perhaps when you've gotten most of the team on board, you'll have to mandate the use of the new technology. Set a target date for 100% usage and make sure everyone knows what it is. When that date comes, rip the band -aid off and insist everyone use the new technology. One organization went so far as to remove the old technology from everyone's computer over the weekend before the 100% go live date. At that point, the staff had no choice. Hopefully, you don't have to implement this step.

Special Pointer for Accounts Payable: We all know that some people fear change. But is it the technology itself that they fear? Although they may find it uncomfortable to learn and how to use it and adapt, that is frequently not the real problem. The elephant in the room, the unspoken concern, is what change the technology will bring and most importantly the negative impact they fear it will have on their job. To put it more bluntly, it is a question of job security.

By understanding this and addressing these fears before they've had a chance to dig their heels in and cause all sorts of trouble, you'll be getting the new technology program off to a strong start.

Worst Practice: Ignoring the situation.

The Issue: Soliciting Process Improvement Recommendations

Many organizations overlook their very best source of process improvement recommendations: the staff who handles the particular function. This is just as true in accounts payable as it is in other functions throughout the organization. However, we're just writing about accounts payable today.

Best Practice: Process improvement suggestions can come from a variety of places. But, an often-over-looked source is the folks who handle the day-to-day work. They are the most knowledgeable when it comes to how the task is done. They can tell you where you can make changes and where the changes you might want to make will not work. While asking the staff for process improvement recommendations is a good idea, it has to be done with care. Sometimes the suggestions offered by the staff will make the accounts payable function more efficient, but will result in problems elsewhere in the accounting chain. Thus it is imperative that the changes proposed be thoroughly analyzed. Then, if the recommendation is a good one, the change needs to be made across the board, with everyone doing the same function making the change.

Almost Best Practice: After you've gone through all the recommendations made by the staff you might want to sit with several processors and watch them go through their work, seeing if you can identify additional points where the process might be able to be improved. This task can be done either by the manager or a consultant or an analyst who works with the staff. Whatever suggestions arise from this exercise need to be vetted by the staff to make sure they are feasible and by a manager to ensure there are no problems created for others working with the information.

Special Pointers for Accounts Payable: Should any of the process improvement suggestions be adopted, they need to be incorporated in the policy and procedures manual. The entire staff needs to be trained using the new process as all should start using it at the same point. If some of the recommendations get turned down, don't take it personally. Remember, there's a big picture and the suggestion must be good for everyone, not just accounts payable.

Worst Practice: Going along using the same processes for year after year without taking the time out to review existing procedures to see if they still make sense and result in an efficient accounts payable function. At a bare minimum, review what you are doing once a year to see if any changes are required.

The Issue: Payment Audits

The issue of payment audits can cause heated debate among professionals in accounts payable. Only about one in three organizations have one of these audits done on a regular basis. A payment audit involves a third-party firm reviewing the payment activity with an eye towards identifying and recovering duplicate and erroneous payments. These audits typically also involve the third party recovering unidentified open credits.

There are many benefits associated with having a payment audit done. Clearly there is the financial gain of the funds recovered during the audit. These are reduced by the contingency percentage typically taken by the audit firm. Additionally, the firm should prepare a management report highlighting any weaknesses in your existing process. This report should be scoured thoroughly and the weak spots identified should be fixed.

Too often people boast that the reason they don't have an audit done is they never make a duplicate payment. Unfortunately, even the best run organization makes a mistake from time to time. What's more, if the person is correct and no duplicate payments are ever made, then the cost for the audit will be minimal, assuming an agency working on a contingency basis is selected.

Another reason people sometimes give for not having an audit done is the expense. They claim the firms charge too much. Let's look at a simple example and see if that theory holds water. Let's assume the audit firm finds and recovers $1 million for the client. In this hypothetical case, the audit firm gets a 25% contingency fee, leaving the client with $750,000 of the $1 million. But, if the firm is not hired, how much will the client recover? How much does it cost not to hire the audit firm? If you are saying nothing, I do not agree. I believe it cost the client $750,000 that will never be recovered unless an audit firm is hired.

This brings up one last issue, or dirty little secret, related to recovery audits. Many people have asked, "well doesn't the vendor return duplicate payments?" And the answer to that question is "most don't." About 1 in 100 vendors will return a duplicate payment without any prompting. The next issue raised is about unclaimed property. And, the answer is yes, the vendor should be turning this money over to the states as part of its unclaimed property reporting – three, four or five years later. However, most don't. They either write it off to miscellaneous income or use it to cover unearned early payment discounts, unauthorized deductions or discrepant invoices. At the end of the day, unless you hire a third party firm or set up a separate unit to recover duplicate and erroneous payments, most of your money held with vendors will be lost.

Best Practice: As suggested above, you can do some easy processes to strip off the low-hanging fruit in terms of duplicate and erroneous payments and open vendor credits. If you have adequate staff, you can request quarterly statements from vendors and recover open credits yourself. Once you've done everything you possibly can, call in the pros and see what they can find. Ideally this should be an ongoing process so the vendors don't have a chance to "use" your open credits to clean up their books.

Almost Best Practice: If you don't have the resources to have a continual audit, try and do it once a year. This is one area where best practices have changed radically. We used to recommend once every two years, but that no longer seems adequate.

Special Pointers for Accounts Payable: Many accounts payable departments are reluctant to have a payment audit done for fear they will be blamed for any funds recovered by the audit firm. This is not fair for often the errors are a result of poor practices elsewhere in the procure-to-pay chain. By getting the management report you will be able to identify these problems. Accounts payable can also make sure that vendors send credit memos directly to accounts payable. Too often they go to purchasing who then throws them away or files them not realizing what they are.

Finally, there is the unclaimed property issue. As mentioned above, these items should be turned over to the state and sometimes they are. In fact, audit firms know that they can start their recovery by reclaiming funds turned over to the state. This is something you can do yourself, assuming you are currently reporting and remitting your organization's unclaimed property. If you are not, filing a claim is like waving a red flag in front of a bull. It will trigger an audit. The amount you recover will be small in comparison to the pain and cost of an audit, when you are not in compliance. Of course, the best practice advice in this arena is to get in compliance. This issue should be kept in mind when hiring the audit firm. If you don't want them recovering funds from the state, tell them this is NOT to be part of the audit.

These will be especially important if you had trouble getting up and running those first few weeks when remote working.

Worst Practice: Not having an audit done because you believe you "never make a duplicate payment."

Inundated with Paper

Chapter 2: Master Vendor File

The master vendor file is critical in the operation of an accounts payable function. When overlooked, poor practices lead to weakened internal controls, potential duplicate payments and the increased possibility of fraud, especially internal fraud. In this chapter we cover the following:

- Who Has Access

- Master Vendor File Set-up
- Using Naming Conventions
- Making Changes to the Master Vendor File
- Master Vendor File Cleanup
- Self-service Master Vendor Files

Issue: Who Has Access to the Master Vendor File

While it is definitely easier for the staff processing invoices for payment if they can add vendors to the master vendor file whenever they get an invoice from a new vendor that practice is an invitation to trouble. Unfortunately, that's how a number of organizations handle information into the master vendor file. This means giving access to the master vendor file to a large number of individuals. This is a terrible idea. It completely disregards the best practice concept inherent in all accounting functions of having appropriate segregation of duties.

Best Practice: Access to the master vendor file, for anything but information lookup, should be severely limited. Only a few people should be able to enter information, be it for setup or to make changes. The employees with this access should not perform any other tasks in the procure-to-pay function making it more difficult for someone to defraud the organization. What's more, when they go on vacation, their passwords and access should not be given to someone else. This will simply muddy the audit trail should there be a problem down the line. A better approach is to set the back-up person up with their own user ID and password and then deactivate those when the person with primary responsibility for the task returns. This is less of a problem in large organizations where there will be several people working on the master vendor file.

Almost Best Practice: This is a black and white issue so there really is no almost best practice. In many organizations there are one or two people with access to the entire accounts payable function. Typically, this is the manager, director or perhaps the Controller. While this is not a good idea, it does solve the problem of an unexpected absence, assuming the person with the broad access is willing to dive in and handle the task. Really, though, unlimited access is not a good idea.

Pointer for Accounts Payable: While limiting access for the purposes of adding new vendors or updating information on existing vendors can seem to make the accounts payable function run less smoothly, it is imperative from an internal control standpoint. Sometimes what is easier for accounts payable is not necessarily good for the organization as a whole and this is one of those instances.

Worst Practices: Worst practices include:

- ✓ Letting each processor update information about their own vendors
- ✓ Letting each processor add vendors whenever it seems necessary

Issue: Master Vendor File Setup

Setting up the master vendor file is one of those functions that no one really focuses on too much. However, handled ineffectually, it can and does lead to duplicate payments and opens the door to fraud. It contains the vital information about a company's vendors. The data contained in each master vendor file will vary from industry to industry. Usually the responsibility for setting up vendors and maintaining them in the master vendor file resides in accounts payable. Sometimes it is in purchasing. Occasionally, each department has its own master vendor file, although this is generally not recommended.

Best Practice: The function should be handled by the organization that can best achieve appropriate segregation of duties. If the staff is small in accounts payable and in purchasing, this might mean the responsibility should reside elsewhere in the accounting function. Vendors should be set up on the master vendor file before any payments are made. Most companies only set companies up if they believe there will be an ongoing relationship with that firm. One-time transactions are typically not set up in the master vendor file, although a sizeable minority does set them up. Information included in the files might include:

- Vendor Name (legal)
- DBA (Doing Business As)

- Business Address
- Ship To Address
- Remit To Address
- Bill To Address (including a contact name)
- Phone number
- Fax Number
- EIN (Employer Identification Number)
- W-9 (on file) Yes NO
- TIN Matching success Yes No (Tax Payer Identification Number)
- For EFT payments: (Electronic Funds Transfer)
- Name on Bank Account
- Bank's Routing Number
- Bank Account Number
- Bank's ACH contact (Automated Clearing House)
- Bank's contact phone number
- Type of business
- Incorporated
- AR contact name, email address and phone number

A form can be used to accumulate this data. Once the information has been compiled, authorized parities should approve (i.e. sign) it.

While most people believe the function belongs in accounts payable, especially when many independent contractors are used, it is acceptable to have it in purchasing, assuming all the rules are followed. Ideally, there should be only one master vendor file.

Each vendor should have one, and only one, master vendor file. When a vendor has several, the door for duplicate payments is swung wide open.

A strict naming convention should be adhered to when setting up master vendor files. While at first glance this may seem silly there are very good reasons for it. For example, a company called The Purple Cafe could be set up as any one of the following:

- The Purple Cafe
- Purple Cafe, The
- Purple Cafe

There is no right or wrong way to set it up – just as long as the leading "The" is always treated in the same manner. Similarly, let's look at IBM to see what could go wrong. Here's a few ways the venerable computer company could be listed:

- IBM
- I B M
- I.B.M.
- International Business Machine

Without a naming convention several files could be set up for the same company. This also makes it difficult for accounts payable associates checking the master vendor file to ascertain if a payment has been made. Which IBM file should they look in?

Here are some guidelines you might use:

✓ Use the initials or acronym rather than the full name of vendors commonly known by their initials or an acronym, i.e. IBM not International Business Machine

✓ Do not use abbreviations except as above, i.e., Olympia & York not O & Y

✓ Use an & for vendors with the word "and" in their name, i.e. D&H not D and H

✓ Eliminate spaces and period between initials, i.e. IBM not I B M or I.B.M.

✓ For individuals use their first name then a space then their last name i.e. Mary Schaeffer not Schaeffer, Mary or Schaeffer Mary

✓ Do not leave a space between Mc (or Mac) in either a company or individual's name, i.e. MacDonald not Mac Donald

Companies typically assign a vendor number to each vendor. Companies also typically include their employees who travel in their vendor files. This is so T&E reimbursement payments can be made. Some use the employees' Social Security number as the employee ID number and in the Master Vendor file. With all the recent problems with identity theft, this once common practice should be eliminated. Employees who regularly receive payments should be assigned a vendor number that is different than the social security number. In fact, some question whether it is necessary to have this information for employees in the vendor file.

As it is often difficult to get W-9 information from independent contractors, making a completed W-9 form part of the process of setting up the master vendor file is a good idea. Without the completed form, the file cannot be set up and consequently the invoice cannot be processed for payment. Establishing the process in this manner takes the pressure out of accounts payable for being the bad guy refusing to make the payment.

Almost Best Practice: Few accounts payable departments have the luxury of starting over with the master vendor file. Occasionally when a new accounting system is put in, companies will take a thorough look at the master vendor file. However, it is never too late to start using best practices and it is never too late to start with a naming convention. This won't help the old data but will get the master vendor file pointed in the right direction.

Pointers for Accounts Payable: Don't fall into the trap of setting up a vendor with the minimum of information just to get the payment made. At the very minimum, insist on getting the W-9 and running it through the IRS TIN Matching program. Periodically, run a report showing all missing information from the Master Vendor File and attempt to fill in those blank spaces.

Worst Practices: Where to start, there are so many? Here's a list of the most egregious:

✓ Not using TIN Matching
✓ Allowing both accounts payable and purchasing each to

have its own master vendor file.
✓ Allowing many people to set up vendors
✓ Allowing many people to change vendor information
✓ Having no naming convention

The Issue: Improve Upfront Vendor Validations for Twenty-first Century Issues

Being thorough when validating new vendors during the setup process will save a lot of headaches if a payment is made that should not have been made. Many companies do not check against the OFAC list or against the addresses in the HR file.

All organizations now have to take care that they do not inadvertently make a payment to a terrorist. It is a fact of life for all organizations making payments, not just those operating in the international arena. Don't think just because the person or entity you are paying doesn't have a foreign-sounding name you are in the clear. You may not be.

All payments should be checked regularly against OFAC's list of Specially Designated Nationals (SDN) before each payment is made. Now, if this seems like a lot of work, you might want to consider one of the vendor portals that checks for you.

Best Practice: As part of the vendor setup routine, check all new vendors against the OFAC list. Additionally, run the vendor's address against the addresses in your HR file to ensure that no employee is trying to set up a phony vendor.

Almost Best Practice: None

Special Pointer for Accounts Payable: Each of these steps can be completed very quickly. It is not a huge change in process to add these to them vendor set up process. Not doing so can result in a lot of explaining, when the company makes a payment it should not have made.

Worst Practice: Not incorporating these simple steps in your new vendor setup process.

Issue: Naming Conventions for the Master Vendor File

One of the reasons that duplicate payments occur is that there is sometimes more than one account set up in the master vendor file for the same company. Consider the case of IBM. Its account in your master vendor file could be called:

- IBM
- International Business Machines
- I.B.M. or
- I B M

Readers probably have additional variations on the few mentioned. If stringent controls are not set around the master vendor file set-up and/or the files are never purged, multiple entries for the same account will ensue. Consider the following very common scenario. The first time an account is set up, it is named IBM. The next time an invoice comes in the accounts payable associate looks for International Business Machines and not finding the entry, sets up another account on the master vendor file using the longer name. Now a third invoice arrives and is paid under the IBM name – but it is paid late so IBM must send along another invoice, marked second notice. The accounts payable associate checks the under the longer name and finding the invoice not paid in that account, goes ahead and pays it.

Hence a duplicate payment is made. Now some reading this may think this is not a big deal; that IBM would probably return the duplicate payment, and in the case of IBM, the duplicate payment would probably eventually be returned – eventually. Researching unidentified cash is never a high priority for overworked suppliers and the funds might not come back for a month. That's one month when the firm wouldn't have use of its money. And, this is the best-case scenario.

In many cases suppliers don't return the funds – that's why duplicate payment audit firms thrive. Suppliers frequently credit the customer's account for the duplicate payment – and leave it there, never alerting the customer to the fact that the account has a credit balance.

Duplicate payments aren't the only potential problem. Multiple entries in the master vendor file open the door for unscrupulous employees to commit fraud.

Best Practice: There is one simple best practice when it comes to master vendor files. Use a standardized set of rules when naming accounts. This is sometimes referred to as naming convention. There is no right or wrong set of rules. The important thing is that there is a standard way to handle the data entry and everyone who enters data into the master vendor file, be it to set up a new vendor or update existing data, use the same standard. This convention should address every single possible issue related to data including:

- ✓ Whether or not to use leading articles
- ✓ Whether or not to include titles
- ✓ Whether or not to use spaces or initials in vendor names that are abbreviated (think IBM)
- ✓ Whether or not to use punctuation in a vendor name (think Macy's)
- ✓ Whether to list independent contractors and employees using the last name first or vice versa

There are a lot more issues. You need to investigate them all taking special care not to include unusual industry specific issues.

Almost Best Practice: There are no almost best practices here. You either use a standardized naming convention or not. A few companies have a few rules regarding naming, addressing issues like the article "The", the use of titles and abbreviations. These are a good start in the right direction but still leave many loopholes open. For the naming convention to truly work it has to be thorough. Otherwise, the door will still be open a crack and the unscrupulous will find ways to smash right through.

Pointer for Accounts Payable: Unless people are intimately aware of the issues relating to names like IBM and the problems they can cause, they will be incredulous when first presented with the standardized rules for naming accounts. Thus, once again, it will fall to the accounts payable manager to educate the rest of the company as to why this is such an important issue. One of the easiest ways to set standards for addresses is to use the standards set by the US post office. They've thought this through, so why not take advantage of their expertise in this arena.

Worst Practices: Worst practices include:

- ✓ Ignoring the issue and having no set of standardized rules.
- ✓ Allowing creativity when it comes to data entry.
- ✓ Not communicating the standards to all affected parties.

The Issue: Contact Information in the Master Vendor File

The reason for this is it is needed for verification purposes any time a request is received regarding the change of a bank account number or the change of a mailing address. It may seem like a lot of work, especially since most of the time when you verify these requests, they will turn out to be legitimate requests. However, the one in 100 times when the request was from a crook and contains a bank account number of someone other than the vendor, the damages can be substantial. These requests are rampant and several companies have fallen for them resulting in losses in the range of six or seven figures

Best Practice: Collect contact information from all new vendors when first setting them up in the master vendor file. This should not be the name and phone number of the sales person but rather someone in accounts receivable and/or treasury.

The contact information should be updated regularly. This is even more difficult as many vendors won't respond to requests for updated contact information. However, given the magnitude of the losses, it is a best practice every organization must seriously consider incorporating into their current processes

Almost Best Practice: If it is not going to be updated periodically, at least collect it when the vendor is first set up.

Special Pointer for Accounts Payable: If the master vendor file doesn't have adequate fields to track this, then keep the information in a separate Excel file or Access database. Not only should this information be collected, it should be very regularly updated.

Too often, when the vendor is set up it is done on a Rush basis because accounts payable only becomes aware that there is a new vendor when an invoice shows up for payment. Then only the information needed to get the payment out the door is collected and the missing information is forgotten. If the vendor is set up in this manner due to expediency, then afterwards an attempt should be made to collect it.

Some best practice organizations routinely review the master vendor file for missing information and attempt to collect it so it will be there when they need it.

Worst Practice: Not collecting contact information at all.

Issue: Updating the Master Vendor File

It would be nice if once a supplier had been set up on the master vendor file that was it. Unfortunately, at least as far as record maintenance is concerned, is that changes occasionally have to be made to the information. People leave, companies move and phone numbers change. Additionally, if terms are included as part of the information in the master vendor file, they too change periodically.

If proper care is not taken with who can make changes to the file and who can't, the company opens itself wide open to fraud. Two simple changes to the "Remit to" address could put a legitimate payment in the hands of a crook, if a company is not careful. An unscrupulous employee with access to the master vendor file would simply change the remit to address for a supplier that is scheduled to receive a large check. After the check is cut and mailed, the employee then makes another change to the remit to address returning it to the correct address. By the time, the supplier complains, the check will have been cashed and it becomes exceedingly difficult to trace the problem. At that point, it would probably be assumed that the check was stolen out of the mail. Who would suspect that someone had fiddled with the master vendor file? It might never even be considered.

Best Practice: Access to the master vendor file, for anything but information lookup, should be severely limited. Only a few people should be able to enter information, be it for setup or to make changes. A form should be used to standardize changes. Changes should also conform to the naming convention used when setting up the master vendor file in the first place. Those who have just read the best practices for setting up a master vendor file will note that there is a bit of overlap when it comes to making changes to the master vendor file. This makes sense. But, do not stop there. There are additional best practices that should be employed when it comes to changes to the master vendor file.

A report should be generated weekly or monthly depending on the number of changes made on average to the master vendor file. The report should detail all the changes made to the file in the given time period. It should include the names of the person requesting the change and the person authorizing the change. It might also include the date the last change was made. This report should be given directly to a senior level executive and should be reviewed line by line for any odd-looking entries. The fact that this report is generated and reviewed should be common knowledge.

In all cases, companies should have the ability to generate this report whenever needed.

Almost Best Practice: While it is desirable that a senior level employee review changes made to the master vendor file, few will be willing to do this. He or she simply does not have the time. They can, however, delegate it to someone on staff.

Pointer for Accounts Payable: In the likely event that the senior executive doesn't review the report, ask that it be given to someone who will.

Worst Practices: Worst practices include:

- ✓ Having no formal process for inputting changes to the master vendor file.
- ✓ Having no review process of the changes made to entries in the master vendor file
- ✓ Having no limits on who can make changes to the file.

Issue: Master Vendor File Cleanup

At many companies, once a vendor gets into its master vendor file it stays there forever. In a perfect world this would not be a problem. However, if an account is not used for a while and then the vendor becomes active, often a new master vendor file is set up. Then, and especially if no strict naming convention is used, there will be two or more master vendor file entries for the same vendor. This can lead to duplicate payments or worse. When a duplicate invoice arrives, and one of the master vendor files checked and no payment is found, a duplicate payment will be made against the second vendor file. Even worse, if an employee bent on fraud becomes aware of an inactive vendor file, the employee can use the inactive file as a cover for fraudulent practices.

Best Practice: Once an account has been inactive for over a year, it should be cleansed from the company's master vendor files – or moved to inactive status. The activity should be maintained for several years. The policy and procedures for master vendor file cleanup should be incorporated into the accounts payable and purchasing formal written policy and procedures guidelines. It is critical that the old data be maintained. In ideal circumstances, the cleansing of the master vendor file is an ongoing task, sometimes performed quarterly.

Maintaining the master vendor file should be an ongoing process and not a one-shot project. The experts like to say that master vendor file maintenance should be a process not a project.

There are certain events that trigger a cleansing of the master vendor file when it hasn't been done in the past. They include, but are not limited to:

✓ The installation of a new accounting package

✓ A merger

✓ An acquisition

✓ The hiring of a new controller or CFO

Take advantage of these events to bring up the issue of master vendor file maintenance and introduce best practices in this area.

Almost Best Practice: If the issue is not going to be addressed on an ongoing basis, the once a year review is probably an acceptable alternative.

Pointer for Accounts Payable: If the master vendor file has never been purged and a new accounting system is being put in place, many companies choose to start over from scratch rather than try and purge the existing file. While this is a lot of work, it is sometimes easier than trying to sort through the mess that currently exists. It is not unusual to hear reports from companies that go through their master vendor file for the first time that indicate the company only kept 30% of the vendors in their old master vendor file.

Sometimes folks will ask what I think of hiring a temp to clean up their master vendor file for them. Because, let's be honest, cleaning up the master vendor file is not a fun job. While they probably could run some reports, at the end of the day, the final review is going to have to be done by someone who knows the business rather well. This means either the accounts payable manager or a seasoned supervisor.

Worst Practices: Worst practices include:

- ✓ Never cleansing the master vendor file
- ✓ Haphazardly cleansing the master vendor file
- ✓ Having no one with direct authority or responsibility for the maintenance of the master vendor file.

Issue: Self-Service Master Vendor Files

Automation has finally found its way into the accounts payable function and master vendor file is no exception. A small but growing number of companies have developed online portals that allow their vendor to input their own information. There's a lot to be said about this approach. First, it gets the vendor to do some of the work and for most organizations that's a plus. But, on the more serious side, it makes the vendor responsible for its own data, including updates. This has become increasingly important given some of the new electronic payment frauds and scams.

Additionally, it makes it easy for the company owning the portal to ping by email their vendors once a year asking them to update contact information. This is a task that rarely gets done with traditional master vendor files. Many who use this type of repository for vendor information find that it creates benefits far beyond those of a traditional master vendor file.

These online vendor portals are quite expensive to build. However, there are alternatives. There are third-party models available for sale and these can be used quite effectively. Some of them will even do TIN Matching and other data verification for you.

Best Practice: Send new vendors a link that provides them access to the vendor portal so they can set up their information in your master vendor portal. These portals are online utilizing a secure connection. Once the information is uploaded someone on staff needs to review it to ensure it conforms to your coding/naming standards. There's no way you are going to get the vendor to enter data according to your standards. If the vendor only adds some of its information but not all, the portal can automatically send reminders asking for the missing information.

As mentioned above, at least once a year an e-mail should be sent to all active vendors asking them to update their contact information. Without this important task the contact information gets stale and within a few years is almost useless.

Most importantly, for those making ACH payments, the vendor is responsible for inputting its bank account information. If it changes bank accounts, it can go in at any point and update its bank account information. That should be the only way that information gets changed. If someone from the vendor contacts your organization asking you to change the data, direct them to the portal. If it is a legitimate call or email, they will make the change appropriately. If it wasn't, you'll have just thwarted a potential fraud.

Almost Best Practice: This is a new area so appropriate practices are still emerging. Use of an online self-service vendor portal is considered a best practice in and of itself. Since organizations utilizing these portals typically are best practice organizations, to date, we haven't seen the emergence of almost or worst best practices.

Pointer for Accounts Payable: Whether you purchase this from a third-party or take the more expensive route of building in-house, these portals are not free or cheap. Hence this probably means a budget item. This means making a presentation to management, demonstrating the benefits and asking for a budget allocation. If you are extremely lucky, you'll present the concept and your company will see the light and give you the okay to go-ahead with either the purchase or development.

However, that is not the likely outcome the first time you bring up the topic. This is something that will have to be talked about for some time. So, get started now. If you are making ACH payments, emphasize the reduction in the fraud risk potential. That can be a huge selling point. As time goes on, we expect this self-service portal approach to vendor information will become more common place.

Worst Practice: So far – NONE. Let's hope it stays that way!

The Issue: Checking for Employees as a Phony Vendors

Unfortunately, from time to time a few unscrupulous employees will try and set up as a phony vendor with an eye towards processing fraudulent invoices for their own benefit. Sometimes they get sloppy and use their own information to do so, making it relatively easy to identify them.

Best Practice: Once a year, the employee address file from HR should be run against the master vendor file to see if there are any duplicate addresses. This run will need to be adjusted if your employees who travel are entered as vendors. Any matches should be thoroughly investigated. Why? The answer is that occasionally an employee will embezzle from his company by submitting phony invoices and having the checks go to his home.

This relatively simple check will help identify those situations where there might be a problem. Obviously, further investigation is needed once a match is found. Of course, if they were smart and used their brother-in-law's address, they would not be so easy to find.

Almost Best Practice: Doing this match when the vendor is first set up and then never again.

Special Pointer for Accounts Payable: Some accounts payable departments also run the TINs in the master vendor file against the social security numbers in the HR file. However, not all HR departments will allow you to do this, citing privacy issues. Likewise, some will run the bank account numbers given for direct deposit of payroll against the numbers provided by vendors for electronic payments, if HR is willing to share that information.

Worst Practice: Assuming all employees are honest and not doing any checking. Sadly, not all are.

The Three-Way Match

Chapter 3: Invoice Processing

Invoice processing is the core of the accounts payable function. Without it, the tasks typically handled in accounts payable could probably be assigned to other units in accounting and purchasing. In this chapter we discuss:

- Receipt of Invoices
- Format for Receipt of Invoices
- Invoice Handling: Approvals
- Invoice Data Requirements
- Verifying Invoice Data
- Invoice-Coding Standards

The Issue: Receipt of Invoices

Receiving invoices in a timely manner is critical to an efficient accounts payable function. Yet, this issue is frequently ignored because it's one of those small matters that those not intimately involved in accounts payable don't realize can have a huge impact. Invoices that are delayed in getting to accounts payable often result in the vendor sending a second invoice. In a best-case scenario, that means extra work for accounts payable in identifying that second invoice and NOT paying it. Unfortunately, a few of those second invoices do get paid and that money is rarely returned without some sort of investigation on the part of the accounts payable staff or its agent. In either case, more work for accounts payable translates into a higher expense for the organization.

Best Practice: Invoices should be received in one centralized location. Traditionally this has meant a post office box, with the mail being delivered to accounts payable for processing. However, some vendors are refusing to mail invoices citing the expense and work associated with that task. They insist on either e-mailing or faxing. Thus, we now have to expand the definition of one centralized location to include an e-mail delivery point and a fax delivery point.

The e-mail address should be a generic address (something like ap@abcompany.com) that can be accessed by several people. The fax number should be for a fax machine that will be used for nothing but the receipt of invoices. Ideally, it should be in a secluded corner in the accounts payable department, as far away from others as possible. This will keep them from being tempted to use the fax, and then inadvertently pick up an invoice or two when retrieving their document.

In some organizations, the purchasing department prefers to receive the invoices first. This can create additional work for accounts payable, especially if some of the approvers are tardy in their reviewing of invoices submitted for payment. The ideal solution to this issue is electronic invoicing, be it a home-grown system, a third-party offering or even invoices e-mailed to the company. With an electronic document, everyone can have access to the invoice almost simultaneously and there is an electronic audit trail showing who got what when – and when an approved invoice was sent to accounts payable for payment.

Almost Best Practice: There are still some organizations, albeit a dwindling number, who still refuse to take invoices by e-mail or fax. For those organizations, one centralized address for the receipt of invoices is suggested. However, they are advised to rethink their position on requiring paper invoices. Paper is disappearing fast and some vendors are starting to charge for sending paper invoices.

Special Pointers for Accounts Payable: By giving several people with access to the e-mail account used to receive invoices, you take the onus off one person. Additionally, there are fewer concerns if the person responsible for retrieving those invoices is unexpectedly absent. Finally, you can get the best of both worlds by combining your fax number with an e-fax facility turning those paper faxes into electronic documents before you ever receive them. This is not an expensive option and is within the financial reach of virtually every organization.

Worst Practice: Having no policy regarding the centralization of the receipt of invoices. While it is not desirable to have purchasing receive invoices first, it is better than having no policy and allowing invoices to be sent wherever the vendor chooses.

The Issue: Format for Receipt of Invoices

Invoices are received in accounts payable departments in a number of different ways, with email being the way the majority of invoices arrive at a company. That being said, postal mail and expedited delivery services (FedEx etc.) also account for a good chunk. In a survey conducted in very early 2020, just before the COVID crisis, it was shown that 27% of all invoices arrive through the post. This is a lot of paper to deal with.

Paper carries with it its own inherent problems. Additionally, as we found out the hard way during COVID, physical delivery of paper invoices during a crisis create additional headaches. When there is an emergency, be it weather-related, a health crisis at the national or international level, or a personal issue, those unexpectedly working remotely will only have access to invoices delivered electronically. This can be via email or through a portal.

Best Practice: Require all invoices to be delivered through an electronic means. This could be email or portal. Anything that makes remote access is possible. In a poll conducted towards the end of the crisis, 71% of the respondents indicated they thought they could get to 95% electronic delivery of invoices. (see graph)

Almost Best Practice: None

Special Pointer for Accounts Payable: Be aware, that even if you aggressively try to get everyone to send invoices electronically, you are not likely to be 100% successful. That being said, it is imperative that you keep the pressure on and try and get the percentage received electronically as high as possible. For there will be another crisis at some point, and the next time, it could be a more serious threat preventing anyone from going into the office to retrieve paper.

With over one-quarter of all invoices currently arriving in a physical form, any sort of a situation requiring people to work remotely for more than a day or two would create havoc with invoice processing of invoices received physically. Thus, it is critical that every organization take a serious look at the way it receives invoices.

Worst Practice: Not addressing this issue

The Issue: Invoice Handling: Approvals

In an ideal world, if all purchase orders are filled out completely and correctly, if receiving thoroughly checks all packing slips and vendors create accurate invoices, the accounts payable department should be able to pay the invoice without input from any other party. However, few companies are at this point. Even at those companies where the documentation is good, management often demands that the original purchaser approve the invoice for payment.

Best Practice: At most companies, only certain people can approve invoices for payment. Most companies limit this ability by rank, job responsibility, type of purchase, and sometimes even the dollar amount. In the best of circumstances, the board of directors should have given these approvers authority and accounts payable should have copies of these board authorizations.

Copies of the list, if it exists in paper format, should be given only to those who need it, and in all cases should be filed away carefully. The list should not be hung on the wall for easy reference or left lying on a desk where anyone walking by could see it and easily make a copy. When the list is updated, as it periodically will be, old copies of the list should be destroyed.

Just because an invoice arrives in accounts payable with a senior executive's signature on it does not mean that the senior executive actually approved the invoice. To protect the accounts payable staff, the department should have signature cards in accounts payable containing the actual signature of anyone authorized to approve invoices. And, it should be the executive's real signature, the one he or she uses every day and not the Sunday-school signature.

More than one executive has taken the time to sign a signature card carefully, when in actuality everything else has an illegible scrawl on it. In these cases, the signature card should have the illegible scrawl, as well or the accounts payable associate might suspect fraud when the signature cards are checked.

We are not suggesting that these cards be checked for every invoice that shows up. However, spot checking once in a while is not a bad idea. And, obviously, if a suspicious-looking signature arrives on an invoice, the signature cards should be checked immediately.

Ideally, invoices will arrive electronically. When an invoice is received electronically, it should be forwarded to accounts payable for processing. Using workflow, the accounts payable department can forward the invoice for approval to the appropriate approver. This is based on information provided on the invoice integrated with the approver list discussed above.

Companies should include in their workflow programming an escalating approval feature. What this means is that if the first approver does not respond within a given timeframe, say five days, the invoice is automatically routed to the next higher approver in that chain of command. This not only takes care of tardy approvers, but also vacations and unexpected absences. It simultaneously creates an audit trail for everyone to see. No longer can purchasing claim it sent an invoice back to accounts payable when it is still in the department.

Finally, the audit trail feature combined with escalating approvals make it far less likely that managers will relegate invoice approval to the bottom of their work – especially when not approving invoices may actually create more work for their immediate supervisors.

Having all invoices come first to accounts payable also introduces another control against employee fraud. Invoices cannot be altered, nor can they show up out of the blue with what looks like an executive's signature on them. By scanning the invoices and forwarding them for approval, it makes it all the harder for a scheming employee to forge a boss's signature.

Almost Best Practice: In the absence of board authorizations, accounts payable should have a list of who can approve what purchases. A high-level executive at the company should sign off on this list.

Special Pointers for Accounts Payable: Be careful of admins who approve for their bosses. While this might make life easier for the boss, it is a complete breakdown of appropriate internal controls and should not be tolerated.

Worst Practice: Worst practices include:

- ✓ Not having a list of authorized approvers
- ✓ Allowing anyone to submit invoices for payment.

The Issue: Invoice Data Requirements

You would think that vendors would instinctively include all information on an invoice needed to get it paid quickly and accurately. But this is an issue many don't take seriously. They send an invoice in for payment with no data indicating who ordered the item. This makes it extremely difficult for accounts payable to get the invoice approved and scheduled for payments. What's more, some of these vague invoices are actually fraud.

Best Practice: Invoices that arrive without the name of the purchaser or a PO number should be returned to the vendor with a polite note stating your organization's requirement that this information be included on all invoices. Otherwise, someone in your organization is going to waste a lot of time trying to figure out who should get the invoice for approval purposes.

Almost Best Practice: To be honest, sometimes it is pretty easy to guess who placed a particular order. If you can tell without too much trouble, it is probably okay to process the invoice without going back to the vendor. However, if you do so, the vendor will never get it right and will continue to send invoices without proper documentation.

Special Pointers for Accounts Payable: While sending invoices lacking the purchaser's name back to suppliers may lead to a smoother accounts payable operation, not all management teams are going to think this is a great idea. Thus, it might be a good idea to get management on board before instituting this policy

Worst Practice: Having no policy on this issue.

The Issue: Verifying Invoice Data

In an ideal world a company would sell its customers products and would in due course be paid for those goods according to the pre-negotiated payment terms, once the purchaser had verified it had received what it had ordered. (Some reading this may recognize this as the underlying principle of Evaluated Receipt Settlement or ERS.) Unfortunately, there is a lot that can and often does go wrong with this simple scenario. Some of the things that go awry include:

- ✓ Terms on the invoice not matching what was negotiated
- ✓ Partial shipments
- ✓ Damaged goods
- ✓ Prices on the invoice not matching the negotiated prices
- ✓ Inclusion or exclusion of related charges such as freight, insurance etc.
- ✓ Sales and use tax charged/not charged

Consequently, the process for paying for goods can be quite complicated – especially when it comes to verifying the suppliers' invoices.

Best Practice: Once an invoice has been approved (if that is required), a three-way match should be performed on all invoices over some minimal level. Small dollar invoices will be addressed further on. The accounts payable associate should match the PO against the invoice and packing slip to verify that the goods ordered have been received and the price and other fees (tax, insurance, freight, etc.) are as agreed.

Differences must be resolved before the invoice can be paid. If the difference is in the pricing, the better price should be taken. If the lower price happens to be on the invoice, not only should the lower price be taken, but purchasing should be also notified. The reasoning for this is that if a lower price is put on an invoice, it probably indicates that the supplier is offering a lower price to other customers and purchasing should pursue that for your company.

Discrepant invoices should be resolved quickly. Ideally, the manager should track all discrepant invoices to make sure that they don't drag on unresolved for months on end.

The process described above can be done online. The best systems now have online dispute resolution features built in – especially when using electronic invoicing.

As alluded to above some companies use a process known as evaluated receipt management (ERS). This eliminates the invoice from the process – the document that many accounts payable professionals believe causes the most problems with the three-way match. Using ERS, the accounts payable staff receives POs from purchasing and when it gets the packing slip from receiving, it pays according to the terms indicated on the PO. Companies that insist that the PO be completely and accurately filled out have taken the first step towards being able to get rid of the invoice. If the PO line is under control and the professionals on the receiving dock thoroughly check the packing slips on incoming orders, a company could effectively use ERS. Use of ERS has to be negotiated with suppliers before implementing. This is also known as pay-on-receipt.

In addition to verifying that the PO matches the invoice regarding price and other fees, many companies are now taking the verification process one step further with a contract management function. As the title implies, invoices, sometimes after the fact, are checked against contracts to ensure that pricing, terms etc. are charged as agreed upon in the master contract agreement. This typically only occurs with major suppliers.

Almost Best Practice: Obviously, going through a thorough three-way match can be an expensive process for small dollar invoices. There is an alternative. First the company must set a dollar cut-off for use of one of the alternatives. This cut-off can be as low as $100 or as high as $5,000 or $25,000. Companies that institute one of the following can start small and then increase the level as they get comfortable with the process. Corporate culture will also have an impact.

The first approach is referred to as negative assurance or assumed receipt. When accounts payable gets an invoice for an amount under the agreed-on level, an e-mail is sent to the person who would approve the invoice indicating key factors, such as payee, dollar amount, etc. If imaging is being used, a copy of the invoice can be attached to the e-mail message. If accounts payable does not hear from the approver within a preset number of days, typically five to ten days, the invoice is paid. The goods are assumed to have been received unless the purchaser notifies accounts payable to the contrary.

Special Pointers for Accounts Payable: Many approvers don't check the information on invoices. Nor do they bother to verify that the invoice they are approving today wasn't approved last week or last month. That's part of the reason so many duplicate payments occur. It's also why the three-way match and ensuring that associated purchase orders and receiving documents are extinguished.

Worst Practice: Simply relying on the approval signature to pay the invoice without verifying the veracity of the information on the invoice.

The Issue: Invoice-Coding Standards

Coding invoices is one of those functions that no one really focuses on too much. However, handled ineffectually, it can and does lead to duplicate payments and opens the door to fraud. It is one of those functions that at first glance, seem like a non-issue. What do you mean you want standards for coding invoices? The words "control freak" may be running through your mind. But consider the following simple case. Consider the company AT&T. Its name could be coded:

✓ American Telegraph and Telephone
✓ AT&T
✓ A T & T
✓ A T and T

Even, if you eliminate the first entry as unlikely, it is easy to see how two competent accounts payable specialists could code the company name in any one of several ways – none of which would be inaccurate. Each data element has similar issues.

Best Practice: Develop a rigid coding standard that addresses every possible issue related to invoice data entry. It should be consistent with your naming convention used for the master vendor file. It should be used by all processors and NO creativity permitted when it comes to data entry.

There is no right or wrong way data should be entered just as long as everyone does it the same. At a minimum your coding standard should address:

✓ How you handle abbreviations

✓ How you handle spaces, periods and other punctuation in a name

✓ Whether you enter an individual's name, first name first or last

When it comes to setting a standard for entering addresses, the easiest way to set this is to rely on the standards set by the US Post Office.

When it comes to entering invoice numbers, special care should be taken, especially if you have only a limited number of fields to enter the invoice number. Do you code leading zeros or not? There is no right or wrong answer to whether or not to code leading zeros. Each company must decide if it wants to code them, and then set a policy. Each aspect of invoice coding policy should be addressed, a policy set and then communicated to all processors. It may seem excessive, but it will eliminate numerous problems down the road.

If you have the space limitation, you will also want to consider whether to eliminate extra digits at the beginning of the invoice number or the end, if you do not have enough space. Most would eliminate leading digits rather than those at the end.

Some with unlimited space rely on the old "key what you see." Don't forget to address any industry peculiar issues you may have.

Almost Best Practices: Almost best practices include:

✓ If no invoicing coding standard exists, use the standard naming convention used when setting up master vendor files. While not perfect – it doesn't address certain issues peculiar to invoices – it is better than nothing.

✓ If an invoice-coding standard does not exist, at a minimum, establish policies for coding the invoice number. If various staffers code invoice numbers differently, duplicates will seep into the process.

Special Pointers for Accounts Payable: Even with a clear policy, processors will occasionally veer off. As soon as this is noticed, the accounts payable manager needs to correct the situation, as without conformity on this issue, duplicate payments will slip through. If the thought process behind the policy is explained, most processors will understand and abide by it.

Worst Practice: Not having a policy at all. Each processor will use his or her best judgment, leading to numerous duplicate payments.

Multiple Copies of The Same Invoice

Chapter 4: Invoice Headaches: The Problem Children Invoices

Unfortunately, invoices rarely arrive in perfect condition. For most companies there are typically problems with the invoice data or data missing from the invoice. That's part of the reason we can't take a "you get an invoice; you pay an invoice" approach to accounts payable. If we took that approach, we'd pay more than we should and some invoices would get paid more than once. In this chapter we discuss:

- Short-Paying Invoices
- Handling Unidentified Invoices
- Handling Invoices without Invoice Numbers
- Discrepant Invoices

The Issue: Short-Paying Invoices

When most companies print their checks, they print identifying information on the accompanying remittance advice. The most important piece of information usually is the invoice number. It gives the vendor the information it needs to apply the cash to the correct account. Certain companies send along a stub with their bills. They require that this stub be returned with the payment. This is so the vendor can apply the cash payment correctly.

However, as those reading this are well aware, the amount of information that can be included on a remittance advice is severely limited. When an invoice is short paid, and the reasons for the short payment are not communicated to the vendor, it is inevitable that the vendor will call accounts payable for an explanation. Unfortunately, by the time the vendor gets around to calling, days, if not weeks will have passed and the accounts payable associate will have long forgotten why the deduction was taken – assuming that the person getting the call was the person responsible for the deduction in the first place.

Deductions are frequently made, for various reasons including:

- ✓ Discounts for early payment
- ✓ Short shipments
- ✓ Damaged goods
- ✓ Advertising allowances
- ✓ Prior credits
- ✓ Insurance or freight incorrectly charged
- ✓ Pricing adjustments
- ✓ Over-shipments
- ✓ Advertising allowances

Best Practice: Whenever invoices are not paid in full, it is important, not only to keep the accounts payable department running smoothly, but also to help maintain good vendor relationships, that the reasons for the deductions be communicated in as much detail as possible to the vendor. This does not ensure that the vendor will agree or won't call, but it will eliminate many needless calls.

Thus, even though it might take a little extra time when the invoices are being processed, put detailed notes in the file as to the reason for the deductions. This can be important if the matter is raised after several months or in the case of an audit. The detailed notes will be worth their weight in gold.

The best approach is to include a detailed breakdown for the reasons for the deductions. Those making electronic payments will find that this information can often be shared as part of the electronic remittance advice. Alternatively, it can be e-mailed to the person at the vendor doing the cash applications. This is extremely important because some vendors refuse to accept electronic payments because of the cash application problems. If you can demonstrate that you've solved this problem, they will be more likely to accept electronic payments from your organization.

Almost Best Practice: A low-tech approach, especially useful with payments made by check is to develop a form listing the most common reasons for short payments. Then the accounts payable associate can simply check off the appropriate field and attach it to the check. These forms should be developed based on the company's past history and industry. They should be periodically reviewed to ensure that they contain all relevant factors. There should be several blank lines at the bottom for any details that will be useful to those using the form.

There is a small group of accounts payable organizations that never short pay an invoice. They hold the view that they will not pay an invoice until it is prepared correctly. They return these invoices demanding that the supplier correct them and when the invoice is prepared satisfactorily, they pay it.

Special Pointer for Accounts Payable: Don't expect that the form will put an end to vendors' complaints. It will simply eliminate one round of calls and one round of investigations as the information typically provided in that round will have been provided on the form.

Worst Practice: Sending along a short payment with no explanation. The vendor will call and even worse, may end up putting the company on credit hold thinking it is owed money. The name of the game in this case is communication – you can't have too much of it.

The Issue: Handling Unidentified Invoices

More often that you'd think, an invoice shows up in the accounts payable department with no identification as to who ordered the product. Occasionally these invoices will float from desk to desk throughout the company before finding their way into accounts payable. Sometimes by looking at what is included on an invoice, a savvy processor will be able to figure out who the likely purchaser is and will then forward the invoice to that person for approval.

However, that is frequently not the case, especially in the case of generic goods like printer cartridges or paper for the copy machine. Often the dollar amount involved is small and does not appear to be worth the time and effort to research who ordered the goods. These are especially problematic as there is a higher incidence of fraud with these invoices than might be expected.

Best Practice: The best approach is to send these unidentified invoices back to the sender asking them to indicate who ordered the goods. To be clear, an unidentified invoice is one that does not have either a purchase order number or name of a requisitioner. Include a polite letter stating that it is your organization's policy to require this information so you may get the invoice paid as quickly as possible. By showing the vendor how they will benefit by including this information, they will be more likely to adapt to your requirements.

By the way, this requirement, as well as any other accounts payable requirement, should be included in your terms and conditions provided to the vendor at the beginning of the relationship. This stance is especially important in the case of small dollar items. (See Worst Practices below).

Almost Best Practice: If it is not feasible to simply return the invoice, pick up the phone and call the vendor. When provided with the information, request that in the future the vendor include the requestors' names on invoices. If this is a recurring problem, keep a list of vendors who routinely omit the purchasers' name along with the employees' names who regularly order from these companies. Again, ask the employees to request that their name or department be included on all invoices.

Special Pointers for Accounts Payable: This is one of those headaches that can be eliminated. Yet, many management teams are reluctant to allow the return of invoices without the information needed. One company that rigidly stuck to this practice reported that within three months, all of its vendors were complying with their requirements. Share this fact with managers who do not want to adopt this practice.

By working with these suppliers, many of whom are small and will be amenable to listening to suggestions (rather than demands); accounts payable will be able to make a serious dent in the problem.

Worst Practice: Simply paying for the goods reasoning that the dollar amount is too small to bother with. This can quickly get your company on the sucker list. More than a few companies out there prey upon overworked accounts payable departments. They send along invoices for goods not ordered, knowing full well that small dollar invoices are often paid without authorization. Once you pay that unidentified invoice once, your company will be hit over and over again – and probably for increasingly larger amounts of money as time goes on.

The Issue: Handling Invoices without Invoice Numbers

Invoice numbers are extremely important when it comes to processing invoices. They are the primary way that most companies identify invoices and check to see if they have already paid a particular item. An invoice without an invoice number is much more likely to be paid twice than one that has this key identifier. Yet a surprisingly large number of invoices routinely arrive without invoice numbers creating all sorts of headaches for the companies that receive them.

That's just the beginning of the problems. When an accounts payable associate goes through its computer files, he or she will search to see if the particular invoice number has been paid. Additionally, most accounting programs require an invoice number in order to generate a payment.

So, to get around these problems, most companies assign invoice numbers to those invoices that arrive without these important identifiers. If not done in a manner that will create unique identifiers, the system will regularly dump out a large number of payments when any duplicate payment check programs are run. The key is to do it in the manner that does not create more problems than it solves.

Best Practice: This is another area where best practice thinking has changed. Today, just about everyone, even the smallest businesses, have access to computers. So, a unique invoice number should be part of your requirements. Take any invoices that arrive without an invoice number and return them to the vendor with a polite note explaining your requirement that every invoice have an invoice number.

Almost Best Practice: The important facet of this discussion is to recognize that invoices without invoice numbers are a problem and to devise a system to deal with the issue that does not create additional problems at the same time. The best technique is probably to make up a dummy number that includes some unique identifier to the vendor, for example, a combination of digits from the vendor's phone number and a running total.

Special Pointers for Accounts Payable: Invoices without invoice numbers create huge headaches in accounts payable. Even if you have a wonderful system for creating an invoice number, that number will not be of any use when discussing open items with the vendor as it does not know the invoice number and if you refer to that identifier, the vendor will have no idea what you are talking about.

Worst Practice: Worst practices include:

- ✓ Using the date to assign an invoice number is likely to cause problems, as you will probably end up with duplicate invoice numbers. Some use a combination of the vendor number and the date. Again, this can cause trouble if you receive more than one invoice from the same vendor on the same day.

- ✓ Creating an invoice number using the account number when it bears any relation to the tax identification number or a person's social security number. There have been instances where unscrupulous employees have taken the social security numbers and used them in an unscrupulous manner.

The Issue: Discrepant Invoices

Discrepant invoices are those that don't match what is on the receiving document and/or purchase order. Many organizations try and resolve these problems before paying the invoice, refusing to make partial payments. This works well in theory but not always in practice.

The most obvious problem is that the invoice problem is not resolved before the due date, thereby making it impossible to pay the invoice on time. Delays in communication and finding the necessary information to resolve the discrepancy are common. Unfortunately, when the invoice is not paid, the vendor often issues a second invoice.

This is not an unreasonable approach on its part. When that second invoice arrives, accounts payable has to identify it as a second invoice. That takes unnecessary time and effort. What's more, some of those second invoices slip through and get paid. This is not a good thing as few duplicate payments are repaid, without some additional work on the part of the customer.

Best Practice: Have a policy requiring all discrepancies be resolved before the due date. While it is fine to have this as a policy, in reality you will still have discrepant invoices on the due date. You need to take steps to keep on top of those issues. The best way to do this is to have the manager track discrepant invoices and follow up with the processor responsible for reconciling the discrepancies on a very regular basis.

Some accounts payable departments regularly produce a report showing the number of discrepant invoices by processor. Some of these reports also age the discrepant invoices. This is one list that no one wants their name on the top of!

Once you have your report of discrepant invoices, probably in Excel format, you might want to add a few columns. You can use these columns to identify the name of the processor, the name of the vendor, the associated purchasing professional and the reason for the discrepancy. If you record all this information on a regular basis, you can use it for analysis once you've collected several months of data.

When you've accumulated enough data, go back and study it to see if you can identify common problems or root causes. For example, if you have an inordinately high number of errors associated with one processor, he or she might need some additional training. If the problem seems to be with a particular vendor, a discussion with that vendor to determine what the problem is might be in order. Your analysis should not be a one-shot deal. You should look at the data every few months. For just as you fix one problem, another is likely to rear its ugly head.

Almost Best Practice: This is an area where there are no almost best practices. Tracking is a must, if you want to keep the discrepant invoice issue under control.

Special Pointers for Accounts Payable: It is imperative that processors keep on top of their discrepant invoices. For without regular follow up, the invoices are apt to languish and those inevitable second invoices will begin to appear. What's more unresolved discrepant invoices have a way of turning into Rush payment requests or even worse, the vendor will use your open credits to clear away the outstanding invoice. While the vendor may think they are doing you a favor, in actuality, they are using your credits to pay for something your organization had no intention of paying for.

Worst Practice: Not tracking discrepant invoices. Without tracking, discrepant invoices end up at the bottom of the pile and contribute to the idea that accounts payable is inefficient.

The Issue: Receiving Emailed Invoices

When invoices are received by email, the invoices are often sent wherever the vendor thinks best. This is often not what is best and results in delays in processing, multiple copies of the same invoice being sent to various parties who eventually forward it (usually) to accounts payable. Without a standard it makes the invoice handling process less efficient than it could be.

Best Practice: Email invoices should be directed to a separate email address set up to receive invoices only.

In no case should this be to an individual, for if that person is unexpectedly absent, the company will be delayed in getting access to the invoice for processing. Also, each processor should not receive invoices in their regular mailbox, mixed in with other email. Since it is quite likely that email will be the primary mode of delivery for invoices in the next few years, it is critical that every organization incorporate this into their everyday practices.

Almost Best Practice: None.

Special Pointer for Accounts Payable: Setting up the email account does not guarantee vendors will use it. Some will persist in sending invoices to people who they "think" will get them priority treatment.

Suggestion: Educate your vendors that sending invoices anywhere but to the email address set up to receive invoices will only delay the processing of their invoice and hence their payment.

Worst Practice: Allowing vendors to email invoices to whomever they wish.

The Issue: Reducing the Number of Multiple Invoice Copies

Technology is generally a plus when it comes to productivity. However, it sometimes brings along with it unintended consequences. That certainly has been the case when it comes to the sending of invoices. Many vendors have discovered that they can send multiple copies of an invoice for virtually no additional cost.

The questionable practice began when vendors would both email and snail mail a copy of the same invoice. That practice persists as does the practice of emailing the same invoice to several people within the organizations. Ask the vendor why they do this and the most common response is that they are just trying to get paid. However, a few customers think the vendor is trying to get them to pay twice.

This practice is exacerbated by a few consultants who urge the clients to improve their cashflow by emailing a second copy of the invoice either on the due date or five days before the due date. Very often these mailings are automated, with the vendor sending the duplicate copies to every single customer with unpaid invoices on their books.

Best Practice: Create procedures for eliminating duplicates including:

- ✓ Identify the culprits and ask them to stop. This step will have to be repeated periodically. Warn them that if the practice continues, you will be forced to double check all their invoices and this could further delay payment.

- ✓ Make sure none of your employees are sabotaging your efforts by asking suppliers to send them a copy also – and then they forward it to accounts payable for payment.

- ✓ Pay on time. Vendors are within their rights to submit a second copy of the invoice, if you haven't paid them within the agreed upon payment terms.

- ✓ Create an automated notification to your vendors telling them you have their invoice. If you can indicate an approximate payment date, do so. It will help to reduce those annoying calls asking when payment will be made.

- ✓ When saving electronic invoice copies, a protocol should be developed so all invoices are saved in the same manner and duplicate invoices are easily caught early in the process. While this will help, it isn't the silver bullet we'd like it to be.

Almost Best Practice: Only use some of the steps discussed above, not all of them.

Special Pointer for Accounts Payable: This problem does not appear to be going away. What's more, in tough economic times, you can expect the problem to be exacerbated, as suppliers become more aggressive in their collection efforts.

Worst Practice: Ignoring the issue

Death by Paper Check

Chapter 5: Checks

Despite the fact that checks are an expensive, inefficient way to make payments, virtually every organization in the United States relies on them heavily to facilitate payments. In most of the rest of the world, payments are largely made electronically. So, we're going on record as noting that electronic payments are a more proficient way to fulfill financial obligations. However, due to their heavy use in the US, we feel it important that we address the issues surrounding them. It is with heavy heart that I report, despite some really innovative changes made by NACHA, the US is a long way from making most B2B payment electronically. In this chapter we discuss best practices related to:

- Approach to Paying by Check
- Check Printing
- Check Signing

- Check Stock Storage
- Distribution of Checks
- Check Fraud
- Use of Payee Name Positive Pay

The Issue: Approach to Paying by Check

As mentioned above, paying by check is a rather inefficient way to pay invoices and other obligations. With the emergence of the ACH in the United States, there is now a low-cost alternative to the paper check nightmare. What's more, not only is it a less expensive approach, it also eliminates certain inefficiencies from accounts payable and solves certain problems.

For example, with no un-cashed checks there is no need to do due diligence on un-cashed checks and then remit the funds to the states as unclaimed property.

Best Practice: Actively encourage all vendors to accept payments electronically or accept p-card payments. Both methods reduce the number of paper checks issued. Develop a plan to systematically approach vendors asking them to accept electronic payments. Do whatever you can to reduce the number of paper checks issued.

Almost Best Practice: If you aren't ready to go full steam ahead with plans to pay vendors electronically, at least pay those vendors electronically who request such payments. And begin to make plans to expand your electronic payment horizons in the near future.

Special Pointers for Accounts Payable: The accounts payable arena is changing and payment methodology is leading the charge. As the number of individuals paying their own personal bills electronically continues to skyrocket, executive reluctance to electronic payments should subside.

Worst Practice: Refusing to pay any vendor in any manner other than with a paper check.

The Issue: Check Printing

Companies print checks as frequently as every day and as infrequently as once or twice a month, depending on numerous factors, which can include:

- ✓ Corporate culture
- ✓ Whether they are trying to encourage vendors to accept electronic payments
- ✓ Cash management practices
- ✓ Number of checks printed
- ✓ Check-signing practices
- ✓ Check-printing practices
- ✓ Efficiencies in the invoice handling procedures

As bizarre as it may seem, a few companies print checks only once or twice a month, not because that is an efficient way for them to run their business but because they feel it gives them greater control over their cash flow. They can tell a vendor that they will print their check at the first opportunity—which will be in two or three weeks in the very next check run. Unfortunately for them, this excuse often ends up with the vendor threatening to put the company on credit hold, which in turn results in manual Rush (and very inefficient) checks. As those familiar with the implications of Rush checks are well aware, this can in turn lead to an increase in duplicate payments and potential fraud.

Obviously, the size of the company and the number of checks it needs to issue will directly affect the frequency of its check runs.

Best Practices: While we might argue that the best practice when it comes to printing checks would be to not print any checks at all—to convert to a 100 percent electronic medium relying on the automated clearinghouse (ACH), this is not a realistic approach at the current time. Given that checks are here at least for the short run, let's take a look at the state of check printing today.

Regardless of the type of printing used (mainframe or laser), AP departments should make sure all affected parties know not only what their check run schedule is but also the cutoff points. If an approved invoice or check request needs to be received in AP by noon on Thursday in order to be included in a Friday check run, this vital information should be shared. Otherwise, people will show up in AP on Friday morning with requests, expecting them to be included in that day's check run. In the long run, it is far better to spend the time communicating this information (verbally, in writing, and on the department's intranet site) with everyone who could possibly be affected.

The process for printing checks in corporate America today is generally handled in one of two ways —either on a mainframe or on a laser printer. Best practices for printing on a mainframe will be discussed later in the chapter. Generally speaking, laser jet printers are now considered the ideal way to print checks, assuming appropriate safeguards are incorporated in the process. For starters, no check stock is required. The best practices for storing check stock are explained in the section under that heading. Some companies use numbered safety paper—a recommended best practice. This paper is numbered and incorporates many safety features. Each piece of paper is sequentially numbered.

A log is kept of the sequentially numbered safety paper. By itself, the paper is worthless. However, with the right software, it can be turned into a valuable commodity—a negotiable check. When it comes time to print checks, the number of checks to be printed should be calculated. The safety paper is removed from the secure location, the first number of the sequentially numbered paper noted, and the checks printed. The last number of the sequentially numbered paper is noted. A calculation should be made, based on the beginning number, the number of checks printed, the ending number, and any ruined sheets of paper, to ascertain that no additional checks were printed. It is especially important to collect any allegedly damaged paper and destroy it.

The number of people who can print checks should be kept to a minimum. The person who prints the checks—usually by controlling the software through user IDs and passwords—should not have access to the check stock. Theoretically, when using a laser printer (which, by the way, are regular laser printers) a check run can be had any time a manual check is requested. Each company must make a determination of whether this is desirable and if it wishes to pursue that course.

When checks are printed on a laser printer, the process usually includes use of a facsimile signature. Typically, this signature is included on a separate plate. Companies take different stances on this plate—some leave them in the printer, while others remove them. If the plate is left in the printer—or is an integral part of the machine—additional care must be taken with the printer. It probably should not be left out on the open floor. Although it is true that in order to actually print a check someone would need access to the software and would need to have a password and user ID, a printer with a facsimile plate could turn a plain piece of paper into a negotiable check. (Remember, checks don't have to be printed on special safety paper, it's just a good idea.)

If preprinted check stock is used, a log similar to the one previously described, should be kept. When it is time to run checks, one of the few approved staffers with access to the check stock closet should get the check stock out. Based on the number of checks that need to be run for each account, the appropriate number of checks should be removed. Some companies have so many different accounts that they end up using a cart to bring the appropriate number of checks for the different accounts to the computer room to be printed. The checks should not be stored in close proximity to the printer—it just makes it too easy for a thief. Typically, someone in Treasury or Accounting will bring the checks up to the Information Technology (IT) department to be run. This representative should watch while the checks are printed.

Since this type of check is typically of a continuous format, it is difficult, if not impossible, to rerun a check (in the same check run) if something goes wrong. When the checks are printed, notations should be made in the log regarding the first check number, the last check number, and the number of checks printed. Both the representative from Accounting (or Treasury) and IT should initial the log.

If a check prints off center, jams, or has some other problem, it should be voided—either by writing VOID across the check in capital letters or by tearing off the MICR (magnetic ink character recognition) line. In any event, all damaged checks should be kept after voiding them. This is to ensure that the checks are actually voided and do not land in the hands of a crook. Also, make sure the appropriate entries are made to your accounting logs or it will look like an un-cashed check that should be turned over to the state as unclaimed property.

Some companies like to have two people present when checks are printed regardless of the methodology. In this case, both should calculate the number of checks used versus the check numbers and initial the log.

Periodically, the log used to verify check counts versus check paper used should be audited—and occasionally on a surprise basis.

At regular intervals, say once every two years, or if there is any significant change in activity (e.g., due to a merger or spin-off), a review of the frequency of check runs should be undertaken. As part of this process, an analysis of the number of rush checks (and the reasons for those requests) should be included. If too many rush checks are required, a company may want to increase the frequency of its check-printing process. If electronic payments continue to increase, many midsize companies may be able to cut back on the number of check runs they have each month. In fact, some will take this step in order to encourage vendors to sign up for electronic payments, which may be issued more frequently, if the company so desires.

Anyone involved in the check-printing process should have no responsibility for reconciling the company's bank accounts.

Once the checks are printed, they should be kept with great care until they are mailed. This means that if they are not mailed the same day they are printed (as they ideally should be); they need to be kept in a secure location. They should not be kept on the credenza of an executive who has to provide a second signature nor lying around the Accounts Payable department. More than one sticky-fingered employee or cleaning person has walked off with a check that did not belong to him or her.

Almost Best Practices: As you can see, especially if preprinted check stock is used, check printing can be a non–value-added, time-intensive task. Some companies choose to outsource this function to their banks. It adds little value and can cause a lot of trouble if not handled correctly.

Some would argue that including any check-printing data about anything other than laser printers in the "Best Practices" section is not appropriate and that printing continuous formatted checks on mainframes is not best practice. They might be correct. However, numerous companies still use continuous formatted checks, so they will be included in that section—at least for now.

Special Pointers for Accounts Payable: With a little bit of luck (okay, maybe a lot of luck) the check-printing function will diminish. For the last few years, the number of checks written has actually decreased. That decrease, at least for the titans of industry, has come through two best practices:

1.   The use of purchase cards (p-cards) and other practices to eliminate small-dollar invoices from the corporate landscape

2.   The move toward electronic payments primarily through the ACH

Thus, check printing may become less of a problem at some point in the future.

Worst Practices: Worst practices include not taking the appropriate steps to guard both the check stock and the check-printing equipment. Several years ago, an auditor noticed that his client had left the check-printing machine out in the open with the signature plate in the machine. Luckily for his client, he was an honest man. To make his point, he printed a check for $1 million made out to himself and left it on the controller's desk with a little note. The controller got the message and made the appropriate changes in the check-printing policies and procedures. Most importantly, a company that does not exercise "reasonable care" in its check-printing procedures could open itself up to incur all losses associated with any check fraud. The worst practices include:

✓   Inappropriate segregation of duties

✓   Not exercising reasonable care in the check-printing process

✓   Not maintaining a log to count the number of checks printed versus authorized

✓   Not storing printed checks carefully before mailing

The Issue: Check Signing

As part of the bill-paying process, checks must be signed. How this is done should depend largely on the up-front controls used to vet the invoice and the approval process. In reality, there is a second component—corporate culture. In theory, if up-front controls for approvals and duplicate-payment checking were perfect, there would be no need for a check to be signed by anything other than a machine. Very few companies, unfortunately, are in a position or are willing to let every payment fly through the invoice-processing cycle without some level of senior checking for high-dollar invoices. The definition of high-dollar invoice varies from company to company.

The information in this section assumes that the company is not using the check-signing process as a checkpoint to catch duplicate and inappropriate/unauthorized payments. If this is the case—and it is a really poor idea—then the company would not want to institute the practices designated in the "Best Practices" section but perhaps some hybrid as defined in the "Almost Best Practices" section.

The Board of Directors should authorize check signers. Alternatively, a senior-level executive who has been delegated by the Board may give others signatory responsibilities. In either event, banks will require signature cards so that they can verify signatures on checks presented for payment. Do not assume from a bank's request for signature cards that it is checking signatures. Banks do not verify signatures. Occasionally, they will spot check the signature on a check or pull a very-large-dollar check to verify the signature. The emphasis here is on the word occasionally. Any company that is counting on its bank to catch fraudulent checks will find itself with a load of bad checks unless it is using positive pay, which is discussed later in this chapter.

Best Practices: The selection of signers should depend on the number of checks that are manually signed as well as the personnel that will be available to actually sign the checks. Signers, however, should be of sufficient stature within the company and should check the documentation that accompanies the check for signature

Most companies put their top-level executives, such as the chief executive officer (CEO), chief financial officer (CFO), and so on, on their bank accounts as signers, even though these individuals rarely sign checks. They should rethink whether this is really necessary. When these officers sign the annual report, they should never use their actual signature. This is for the company's protection and the protection of the officers personally. In the early days of check fraud, thieves simply got a copy of the company's annual report to get a legitimate signature to use in their crooked check activities. Since these executives rarely sign checks, it is recommended that they not be included as signers on bank accounts.

Most companies today use a mechanized check-signing procedure that is integrated with the check-printing cycle. Depending on the dollar amount of the check, the mechanized signature can be the only signature or the first signature. If a mechanized process is used, the signature plate needs to be maintained with proper care and controls. This means it should be easily separated from the machine (computer) that prints the check, or, if it is not removed, the check-printing computer should be kept in a secure location with controlled access. The signature plate, or the machine with the plate in it, needs to be kept in a secure location with limited access. Many companies keep the signature plate used for facsimile signatures in a safe.

Even if up-front controls are airtight, many companies will require two signatures on checks over a certain level. The level will depend on the nature of the business and corporate culture. A smaller company might require the second signature for all checks over $25,000, while a Fortune 50 company might set that level at $1 million. The level reflects the company's comfort level with its invoice-processing controls.

There is a lot of debate over whether a warning should be printed on the checks indicating the level where two signatures are required. This is similar to the warning regarding the maximum dollar amount for which a check can be written. Some believe that putting a notice on the check stating "Checks over $25,000 require two signatures" is a good idea as it alerts the teller of a possible fraud. Others rightly note that such indicator is likely to be of more use to a crook than to the teller. A crook noting such a warning will simply alter the check to no more than $24,999.

Most AP and Treasury groups at large companies keep a list of bank accounts and authorized signers. This is a good idea as long as proper care is taken with these reports. They should be limited in number and given only to those employees who need the information—definitely a need-to-know report. When the report is updated, the old reports should be collected and destroyed. Employees who receive the report should keep it in their desks, not lying on top for easy access.

In no case should anyone who is an authorized signer on any account do bank account reconciliations.

When manual signatures are used on checks, the responsibility for getting the signatures (a truly thankless task) should be given to someone other than the person who prepares the checks.

When the check is given to the signer for signature, all the appropriate backup should be attached and the signer should verify that

- ✓ The check is actually for the invoices presented.
- ✓ The appropriate approvals are in place.
- ✓ The check is drawn on the correct account.
- ✓ The check is for the correct amount.

If the signer is not willing or capable of this verification process, he or she should not be an authorized signer.

Periodically, spot check checks automatically signed to verify quality control.

Almost Best Practices: When companies are not comfortable letting checks go without a senior-level review, the dollar amount where automated signing is acceptable is usually set quite low. Rather than fighting City Hall, AP can suggest that the level be gradually raised. As comfort is gained, the levels can be periodically raised.

Another way to address the issue of having too many checks is to look for ways to eliminate checks, especially checks for low-dollar purchases. Use of p-cards, electronic payments through the ACH, and direct deposit for travel and entertainment (T&E) reimbursements will help address the issue.

Special Pointers for Accounts Payable: Despite their best intentions, few authorized signers will actually go through the appropriate verification process before signing a check. The bulk of the responsibility for those tasks still lies with the AP staff, and if there is an error, it is rarely the signer who is held responsible.

Worst Practices: Worst practices include:

- ✓ Signing checks with a rubber stamp. Although the ease with which checks can be signed with a rubber stamp is appealing to many, it has serious drawbacks. It is so easy for a thief to copy a signature made with a rubber stamp that a company that uses a rubber stamp to sign its checks is not considered to be using ordinary care. The implications of not using ordinary care mean that should any check fraud happen; the company would be liable for 100 percent of the loss.

- ✓ Some companies, thinking they are improving controls, set the dollar level at which hand signatures are required very low. When an executive is presented with many checks to sign at one time, it is unlikely that he will give each an adequate review. Rather than set the dollar level low, it is far better to set it higher, have fewer checks representing higher dollar invoices undergo a thorough review.

The Issue: Check Stock Storage

Blank checks may look innocuous enough, but in the wrong hands they can cause a lot of damage. A thief, disgruntled employee, or even just an inexperienced staffer can cause untold trouble by misusing company checks. In the past, banks ate the losses associated with check fraud. This is no longer the case. They just can't afford these hits to their bottom line. Often, this is an area that is overlooked—no one gives it much thought. However, with all the attention of the recent accounting scandals, the enactment of the Sarbanes-Oxley Act, and the new emphasis on internal controls, how a company stores its checks is likely to come under increased scrutiny.

Best Practices: In the "Check Printing" section, there was a discussion of both laser checks printed on safety paper and preprinted checks. While this discussion does cover both types, it applies to preprinted checks to a larger degree, as that is where the real risk lies.

- ✓ Checks should be stored in a secure, locked location.

- ✓ Access to the check stock should be severely limited.

- ✓ The closet should be reinforced—and not of the type that a crook could easily hack into.

- ✓ The lock on the door should be substantial and not easily picked with a hairpin or clothes hanger.

Ideally, the check storage closet should not be in close proximity to the printer. If someone breaks in, especially on a long weekend, don't make it too easy for him or her.

Sufficient segregation of duties should be incorporated into the various tasks associated with the check production cycle, so the individuals with access to the check storage closet do not also have the authority to print checks. Clearly, anyone with access to the check storage closet should not be responsible for the reconciliation of the company's bank accounts.

Almost Best Practices: When it comes to storing of checks, there is not much give and take. It is something that a company really needs to do right—the consequences of doing it wrong are too great. Therefore, best practices should be employed.

Special Pointers for Accounts Payable: The check stock storage issue is likely to be a touchy issue at some smaller midsize companies. If the check stock or a spare checkbook has always been kept in the assistant controller's office, he or she may be insulted at the suggestion that it really should be moved to a more secure location. This is an internal controls issue and if necessary, the auditors should be asked to weigh in on the issue.

Worst Practices: Worst practices include:

- ✓ Keeping a spare checkbook around, in someone's desk, for those after-hour emergency situations

✓ Keeping checks in the bottom drawer of a filing cabinet, especially if that cabinet is often open and unattended for long periods of time

✓ Storing the check printer (and signature plate) in the same locked room as the check stock

✓ Not adequately segregating duties when it comes to check printing, storage, and the reconciliation of bank accounts

The Issue: Distribution of Checks

Once a check is printed and signed, it has to get in the hands of the payee. The normal way that this is handled is to mail the check to the payee. In fact, some may wonder why there is a separate section for this topic. The answer is that sometimes the person requesting the check will request that the check be returned to him or her for final distribution. Typically, there are three reasons that this request is made:

1. The requestor wants to make sure that the check is mailed correctly.

2. The requestor is a salesperson who wants to deliver the check to the customer and try and pick up another order at the same time.

3. The requestor has some other business relationship with the payee and wants to solidify that relationship.

While the reasons may appear reasonable at first glance, they are overridden by several other concerns, including the following:

✓ It is extremely inefficient and time consuming to return checks to the requestor. Few people outside Accounts Payable realize how disruptive the practice is.

✓ The door for employee fraud is opened wide whenever checks are returned to anyone other than the payee.

✓ Checks returned to the requestors are sometimes lost, misplaced, or not delivered for a long time, often resulting in duplicate payments.

Best Practices: When an invoice is approved for payment, the invoice should have a mailing address on it. Additionally, this address should match the Pay-To address in the master vendor file. Any variation from this should be investigated because it may be the first sign that something is amiss. Under all but the most extenuating circumstances, checks should be mailed.

When checks are mailed, care should be taken regarding when and how this is done. Checks should be sealed in envelopes and delivered either straight to the post office or to the mailroom at the end of the day.

If checks are delivered to the mailroom, they should not be left out in the open where anyone walking by can see them and easily filch one. This is especially true if temporary employees are frequently used.

Similarly, thought should be given as to whether a window envelope should be used. While window envelopes simplify the mailing of checks, they are also a red flag for a crook looking for checks to steal. Rarely are checks mailed in anything other than window envelopes.

Additionally, if one-part sealers (those multipart forms that contain the check) are used, extra care should be taken in the mailing procedures. Again, they are often a red flag to crooks looking for checks.

Almost Best Practices: Sometimes, either the corporate culture or the nature of the business will require the hand delivery of checks, either to company employees or to the customers' representatives. In these cases, to avoid disrupting the AP department too much, the pickup time should be limited to certain days and hours.

A log should be kept for checks not mailed. Each time a check is picked up, the following information should be noted in the log:

- ✓ Check number
- ✓ Payee
- ✓ Dollar amount
- ✓ Date the check was issued
- ✓ Date the check was picked up

✓   Name of the person picking the check up

The person picking up the check should sign each of the entries. Of course, the list of who can pick up checks should also be limited.

Although companies often tolerate the practice of not mailing checks directly to the payee, it should be discouraged. Anytime someone requests that a check be returned, ask why he or she needs it and then point out the advantages of not returning the check.

Requiring an extra level of approval for returned checks will sometimes put a damper on these requests.

Paying customers electronically eliminates this issue!

Special Pointers for Accounts Payable: If the company tolerates the practice of individuals picking up checks, there will be occasions when AP will have to make these checks available outside of the preset hours. This practice should be discouraged as much as possible.

If checks are to be regularly segregated for delivery rather than mailing, firm policies and procedures should be written to govern the process.

Worst Practices: Worst practices include the returning of checks to anyone other than the payee, especially if the person who approved the invoice for payment is the individual to whom the check is returned.

Although circumstances may dictate the issuing of a manual check and returning it to the individual who approved the payment, these should be limited.

The Issue: Check Fraud

Although no one knows the true level of check fraud, most experts estimate that it is at least a $10 billion-a-year business. In years gone by, banks would eat the losses associated with check fraud for their corporate clients. This has become prohibitively expensive, and banks are no longer willing or able to absorb these often-unnecessary expenses. Changes to the Uniform Commercial Code (UCC) have introduced the concepts of reasonable care and comparative culpability.

In plain English this means the person in the best position to prevent the crime will be held responsible. This is done on a pro-rata basis, although there are some things that companies do that place the responsibility 100 percent on their plate. A simple example of this is using a rubber stamp (not a facsimile signer) to sign checks and not keeping check stock in a secure location.

Those who are interested in reading the statutes that cover payment fraud–related issues can refer to:

- ✓ UCC3 for ordinary care
- ✓ UCC4 for reasonable notification
- ✓ UCC4A for acceptable security procedures
- ✓ Regulation CC for shortened return/hold times
- ✓ The National Automated Clearing House Association (NACHA) for unauthorized entries return
- ✓ Certain state statutes

The states have also changed their laws so that companies that fail to exercise "reasonable care" are now allocated the losses associated with check fraud.

It should be noted that despite the growth and publicity around cyber fraud, check fraud remains the most commonly attempted type of payment fraud in the US. Luckily, companies have gotten quite good at combatting it.

Best Practices: While at first blush making all payments electronically might seem to eliminate the problem, it is not practical in today's environment. Numerous companies are not able to take this step, and even more limiting is the fact that a number of their customers are not yet ready to accept payments electronically.

A reasonable best practice for companies is to move as many of their customers to an electronic payment mechanism as possible. In most instances this will require a renegotiation of the payment terms to make the transaction float neutral. If a customer sees the move toward electronic payments as an attempt on the part of the vendor to improve its position, it is unlikely to agree to pay electronically. In a float-neutral situation, both parties still benefit from improved efficiencies and reduced costs.

In addition to positive pay discussed below, companies also need to focus on the check itself. The check should contain some (but not necessarily all) of the following security features:

✓ Watermarks. Watermarks are subtle designs of a logo or other image. Designed to foil copiers and scanners that operate by imaging at right angles (90 degrees), watermarks are viewed by holding a check at a 45-degree angle.

✓ Microprinting. A word or a phrase is printed on the check so small that to the eye it appears as a solid line. When magnified or viewed closely, the word or phrase will become apparent. Copiers and scanners can't reproduce at this level of detail, so microprinting when copied will appear as a solid line.

✓ Laid lines. Laid lines are unevenly spaced lines that appear on the back of a check and are part of the check paper. This design makes it difficult to cut and paste information such as payee name and dollar amount without detection.

✓ Reactive safety paper. This paper combats erasure and chemical alteration by "bleeding" when a forger tries to erase or chemically alter information on the check, leaving the check discolored.

✓ Special inks. These are highly reactive inks that discolor when they come into contact with erasure chemical solvents.

✓ Color prismatic printing. This type of printing creates a multicolor pantograph background that is extremely difficult to duplicate when using a color copier or scanner.

✓ Special borders. These borders on the check have intricate designs that, if copied, become distorted images.

✓ Warning bands. Warning bands describe the security features present on a check. These bands alert bank tellers or store clerks to inspect the check before accepting it. They may also act as a deterrent to criminals.

✓ Thermochromic inks. These are special, colored inks that are sensitive to human touch and, when activated, either change color or disappear.

✓ Toner grip. This is a special coating on the check paper that provides maximum adhesion of the MICR toner to the check paper. This helps prevent the alteration of payee or dollar amount by making erasure or removal of information more difficult.

Pre-printed check stock should not be ordered from a printer but rather printed on safety paper as needed. This means that all the controls surrounding check stock become irrelevant because the only thing the company has ordered is blank paper. The appropriate controls need to be with the software and hardware used to print the checks.

Almost Best Practices: Not every company is willing or able to walk away from preprinted check stock. If the company does use preprinted check stock, appropriate care must be taken to ensure that checks are stored under lock and key and access to the storage area is limited. Additionally, anyone who is an authorized signer or has access to the safe where the signature plates for the check-signing machine (or computer) are kept should not have access to the check stock.

Special Pointers for Accounts Payable: Some companies are very attached to preprinted checks. It is up to the AP executives at these companies to make sure that adequate controls are used with regard to the check stock. Occasionally, organizations will come to the conclusion that because of the move to electronic payments, they can let their guard down when it comes to protections against check fraud. This can lead to disaster. Recent statistics from the Association of Financial Professionals reveal that check fraud is still the most common type of attempted payment fraud. The emphasis is on the word "attempted." For if the proper precautions are taken, these crooks won't be successful. Let up your guard and you'll find they are walking off with your organization's money.

Worst Practices: Worst practices include:

✓ Not using positive pay

✓ Not keeping checks in a secure location

✓ Not incorporating fraud prevention features in check stock

✓ Using a rubber stamp to sign checks

The Issue: Use of Payee Name Positive Pay

A few years ago, the use of positive pay was seen as a leading-edge technique to limit check fraud. Today, it should be part of the payment process at every company. Some think that in a few short years not using positive pay will be seen as not exercising reasonable care. Positive pay is a service offered by most banks. As part of the service, companies transmit to their banks their check issuance file each time checks are written. The file contains a list of check numbers and dollar amounts. When a check is presented for payment, it is matched against the file. If there is a match, the check is honored and the check number removed from the file. It there is no match, the check is handled according to the preset instructions from the company. This may mean automatically rejecting the item, but more likely it means notifying the company and giving it a few hours to send instructions on how the item should be handled. What has been described so far is the basic positive pay service.

A more recent innovation in the area of positive pay is the development of a more advanced product called payee name positive pay. As you might expect, this includes the payee's name along with the check number and dollar amount in the file sent to the bank.

Companies should contact their bankers for the details of the products offered.

While use of the positive pay service is definitely a best practice, some companies have trouble transmitting an issue tape to the bank. For these companies, reverse positive pay is a reasonable option, while they try and alleviate the situation that prevents them from giving the bank a check issuance tape. In this case the bank will transmit a file to the company containing all the checks clearing against the company's account that morning. The company is then responsible for reviewing the information within a few hours and contacting the bank about any that should not be honored. Alternatively, the company can make arrangements with the bank that it honor all checks unless notified.

Best Practice: Use payee name positive pay wherever available. This is your best protection against check fraud.

Almost Best Practice: Use of positive pay, if payee name positive pay is not available. If the organization does not have the ability to create a positive pay file, then reverse positive pay is the best option. Basically, this requires the organization to verify checks clearing each day. It is the organization's responsibility to notify the bank of any unauthorized checks. If they forget or someone is out, the bank is off the hook, if there is a check fraud. Verifying on a daily basis effectively means the task of bank reconciliations is done daily rather than monthly. Additionally, as will be discussed in chapter on Fraud, daily bank reconciliations are recommended as a way of guarding against unauthorized ACH transactions.

Special Pointers for Accounts Payable: Accounts Payable often has a hard time convincing management that positive pay should be used. Don't let this issue drop. While positive pay or payee name positive pay will protect your organization against check fraud that is all it will protect against. It will not protect against other types of payment fraud. Thus, it is imperative that other steps be taken in the battle against payment fraud, with positive pay being just one weapon in your arsenal of defense against the fraudsters trying to defraud your organization.

Worst Practice: Not using any type of positive pay at all.

Paper Check Headaches

Chapter 6: ACH (Electronic Payments)

Electronic payments have long been the norm in parts of the world outside the US. Now, organizations of all sizes and types within the US are starting to take advantage of electronic payments, also referred to as ACH payments or direct payments, to pay their vendors. Most organizations rely on the ACH for their direct deposit of payroll payments. Now, they are taking that approach one step further, using the ACH to pay vendors. The terminology of "direct payment" is a nod toward direct deposit of payroll. In this chapter, best practices related to the following are discussed:

- Approach to Paying Electronically
- Converting Vendors to ACH Payments
- Handling Change of Bank Account Requests
- Convincing Vendors to Convert
- Handling Remittance Information

The Issue: Approach to Paying Electronically

By now, you probably realize I strongly believe in paying electronically instead of using paper checks. The issue is how to get from point A (the paper check world) to point B (an electronic payment arena). The obvious answer is that you can't do it all at once. Many of your vendors won't have the ability to accept electronic payments and apply cash correctly and your own staff is probably not capable of converting the entire vendor base in one fell swoop.

Keep in mind that as the business and accounts payable world is changing, one of the big areas is the use of technology and automation in accounts payable. This includes paying electronically. Even if you don't believe your organization will ever make this move, you may find yourself forced into the electronic payment world when a large supplier dictates electronic payments or taking your business elsewhere. It's the wave of the future, so stop trying to fight City Hall.

Best Practice: Consider moving towards making electronic payments, if you have not already started and if you have, considered increasing the number of vendors paid in this manner. Not only is it more efficient for the accounts payable staff, it is less costly.

The first step in moving into the electronic payment world is getting your own house in order. This means making the necessary changes to procedures and systems to allow electronic payments to be made. It also means getting everyone on board in-house. This would include both management and the purchasing staff. By explaining the benefits to them, they are less likely to object and might even become missionaries advocating for electronic payments instead of paper checks.

Almost Best Practice: If you are not ready to make a full-court press into the electronic payment world, consider at least paying those vendors who request electronic payments. This will enable you to dip your foot into the electronic payment waters without making a full-fledge commitment. It is also likely that the vendor will understand if there are a few snafus in the beginning. This is a great way to get started. Once you have been successful with a few electronic payments, you'll look for ways to increase your participation.

Special Pointers for Accounts Payable: Be aware that there is a cash flow impact associated with making electronic payments. Let me give you a simple example. If you are paying vendors with paper checks that are typically mailed on Fridays, you can probably predict with great certainty when most will clear the bank. You might end up with 10% clearing on Monday, 50% clearing on Tuesday, 30% clearing on Wednesday and the rest trailing in over the next few days. Your cash forecasting folks probably have this built into their cash flow model.

Now, if you move to electronic payments, 100% of your transactions will clear on Monday. This shouldn't deter you from making them, but you do need to factor this into the process. More than a few accounts payable staffs have ended up with egg on their faces when they went full-throttle ahead launching a big electronic payment program.

There are two ways to deal with this issue. The first is to renegotiate payment terms with your vendors to make the transactions float neutral. This typically means adding one or two days to the payment terms. However, this is not always possible. If the vendor doesn't really care whether it is paid electronically, you don't have as much leverage. Despite the vendors' refusal to negotiate terms, it is still recommended you go the electronic payment route. That's because even without the extra days, you are still better off paying electronically than with a paper check.

Worst Practice: Absolutely refusing to pay anyone electronically.

The Issue: Converting Vendors to ACH Payments

There's a bit of work involved converting vendors from paper checks to receiving ACH payments. Deciding that you will pay this way is just the first step.

Best Practice: Develop a systematized approach to converting vendors to electronic payments. Start with a beta or test group. This might be comprised of transactions between various company entities, or it might be trusted vendors who won't complain if the payments don't go as planned the first time out. Don't overlook those vendors clamoring to be paid electronically. All these groups will be less critical should something go wrong than your vendor population at large. You can also try a second beta group consisting of employees being reimbursed for travel and entertainment expenses.

Once you've got your beta group and run a few payments through, review what happened and adjust your procedures to address any rough spots. When you are confident that you have everything working well, it's time to roll your program out to your entire vendor base. But don't do it all at once. One company sent letters to all their vendors expecting a tepid response. When over 25% responded affirmatively, they could not handle the demand and ended up hurting their relations with vendors who were not accommodated. Figure out how many vendors your staff can comfortably convert and make your pitch accordingly. Once you have the first group of positive respondents converted completely, send out your solicitation to your next group. Proceed like this until you have contacted all your vendors at least once.

If your process takes more than six months, when you finish, start again approaching those vendors who turned you down the first time.

Almost Best Practice: As above, pay only those who request electronic payments until you are comfortable with the process. Then go full-steam ahead, approaching all your vendors systematically, as described above.

Special Pointers for Accounts Payable: No matter how hard you try, you will have some vendors who just refuse to convert. Consider paying less frequently with checks than electronically. For example, you might make electronic payments three times a week but only have one check run each week, or even every two weeks. Additionally, insist that all Rush payments be made using electronic payments. Sometimes it just takes one payment for the vendor to see the light.

Worst Practice: Refusing to pay any vendor electronically.

The Issue: Handling Change of Bank Account Requests

Organizations change bank accounts all the time for a variety of reasons. Many times the old account is closed. Sometimes the company has changed its legal structure, sometimes it has changed banks. Occasionally, a fraud has occurred necessitating the change of account. Whatever the reason, when the change is made, if the organization has been receiving payments electronically, they notify their customers of their new account. Most often, notification of this change comes in the form of an e-mail.

Unfortunately, crooks, often quite sophisticated in the use of the Internet, realize this is a potential gold mine. They spend a bit of time analyzing potential targets and creating quite legitimate looking e-mails. These emails purport to come from the vendor, notify customers of a change in the account where payments are being sent. As you might expect, the new bank account is one they control. Once money is sent to the account, it is quickly transferred out of the country making recovery difficult. Regrettably, if your company falls victim to such an e-mail it will still be on the hook for the payment.

Don't be fooled because the e-mail either looks legitimate or looks like it came from the vendor's e-mail account. Really smart IT folks can make the message look like it originated at the vendor's ISP.

Best Practice: Call company to verify the change request. For this to work, you need to have good contact information on hand. This means getting good contact information when you first set up the vendor and then updating it on a regular basis. Whether you keep it in your master vendor file or elsewhere is not important. What matters is that you get the information and keep it updated.

Too often, the only information companies have on hand is the Remit-To address, often a bank lockbox and the salesperson's name and phone number. Neither of these is apt to be much help when trying to verify a change in bank account request. One last note on this point. Whatever means you take to verify the request do not use the contact information contained in the original email request. If it came from a fraudster, they will confirm the information in the phony email.

Some companies are now taking this one step further, requiring employees to start at the vendor website and obtain the general phone number. They then must call the general number and ask to be transferred to Treasury or AR or billing until they get someone who can confirm the request.

Almost Best Practice: A few organizations now require that anyone requesting such a change not only supply the new bank account number but the old bank account number as well. Some also require data on the last three transactions, or other information only the supplier would have. This makes it much more difficult, but not impossible, for a crook to perpetrate this type of fraud.

Special Pointers for Accounts Payable: This type of fraud is expected to grow in the coming years. It is a variant on the change of remit-to address letters crooks sometimes send. Those too should be verified, again, using information you have on hand, not information included with the request.

It was hoped that use of automated self-service vendor portals, where the vendor is responsible for inputting its data, including bank account information for electronic payments <u>and</u> any changes to that information, would take hold. This would remove the onus from the customers. There has been tremendous pushback from the vendor community on this issue, as the self-service portals create a ton of extra work for the supplier. This no longer seems like it will be the silver bullet we hoped for and accounts payable departments cannot rely on this.

Criminals perpetrating this type of fraud are often quite smart. They will send emails asking for the change at a time they know the accounts payable staff is busy. This might be later on a Friday afternoon or at the end of the month. They use spoofed emails or URLs with one letter changed. Be careful.

Worst Practice: Just following the instructions in the e-mail or the letter without doing any verification that the request is legitimate. Equally bad is calling the phone number provided in the e-mail to verify the request. If it is a phony request the person who answers the phone at the number provided will verify it is legitimate, when of course it is not. This is why keeping current contact information is so important.

The Issue: Convincing Vendors to Convert

Converting vendors to ACH payments unfortunately takes a lot more than just deciding this is what you want to do. Unfortunately, you also have to convince your vendors that this is a good approach for them as well. Some will immediately see the benefit while others will drag their feet. But paper checks are just inefficient and best-practice companies everywhere are looking for ways to minimize the number they must issue. What's more, outside the US, most companies use very few checks. Other countries have relied on electronic payments for eons—and they work!

Best Practice: Actively work to convert vendors to your electronic payment program. You can do many things to encourage this conversion including:

- ✓ Explaining the benefits to them (not to you—they don't really care about that)
- ✓ Paying more frequently with electronic payments than paper checks
- ✓ Reducing the number of check runs
- ✓ Paying electronically the day before you release paper checks
- ✓ Keep track of those vendors who seem to be on the fence and re-solicit them every six months

Almost Best Practice: Paying electronically only those vendors who request electronic payments. While this is a good way to dip your feet in the electronic payment waters and get used to the process, it should be done only for a short period of time. Then, the hope is your organization will realize the benefits of paying electronically and flip into the best practice mode.

Special Pointers for Accounts Payable: If you are very serious about converting as many vendors as possible, insist that all Rush payments be made electronically. There are two benefits to this approach. First, it is easier for accounts payable and removes the request for the return of the check to the requisitioner, which happens frequently with Rush or ASAP payments. And second, it introduces the vendor to the concept of accepting electronic payments. Many will find they like getting paid this way and sign up to receive payments in this manner in the future.

Don't assume you'll immediately need fewer staff as you get rid of paper checks. That's true eventually, especially if you have a particularly manual process and are getting hand signatures on more than a few checks. But it will take some effort to handle the conversion so initially you will not have staff to redeploy to more value-added tasks. However, eventually when you've gotten over the hump of converting most of the suppliers who are willing to take electronic payments, you will be able to free up some of your resources.

In the last year or two, there has been an aggressive use of paying less frequently with paper checks than with electronic payments.

Worst Practice: Refusing to pay any vendors electronically. This sticking-your-head-in-the-sand approach is not likely to work for long as more and more organizations see the benefits of being paid electronically. Eventually, every organization will have to do this as 800-pound-gorilla suppliers demand electronic payment. So, why fight this losing battle?

The Issue: Handling Remittance Information

On the face of it, you'd think every supplier would be clamoring for electronic payments. Yet, some refuse to accept them. While at first this seems counterintuitive, there is a good reason for this reluctance. Their cash application folks have difficulty applying cash without that all-important remittance information. If this hurdle can be overcome, many are all too happy to get onboard accepting electronic payments.

Best Practice: Create a separate e-mail with all the remittance information and e-mail it to the appropriate accounts receivable or cash application person at your vendors. This will provide them the information needed to apply cash correctly and should remove what is hopefully the last obstacle to their accepting electronic payments. What's more, if you are able to provide this information a day or two in advance of the payment, it might also help with their short-term cash forecasting—another side benefit.

Almost Best Practice: Mailing the remittance information after the fact. While this is better than nothing, it does take away some of the cost savings associated with the move to electronic payments.

Special Pointers for Accounts Payable: A side benefit of this approach is that you will be forced to keep updated information for the accounts receivable staff. This is something that is recommended as part of a fraud prevention program to help protect the organization against certain types of electronic payment fraud. By collecting the current contact information for remittance advices, you will be one step ahead on that front in your fraud prevention/detection initiatives.

Worst Practice: Ignoring the issue of remittance advices. Even if your vendor is willing to accept payments electronically without remittance information, you are putting your organization at the mercy of their cash application person. Typically, without other instructions, they will apply whatever cash comes in to the oldest outstanding invoice. This may not be what you intended. For example, it could be a disputed invoice that you have no intention of paying. Hence, it is critical that remittance information be included so the supplier knows precisely what you intended to pay with the payment in question.

Tardy Approvals

Chapter 7: An Effective P-card Program

P-cards, also sometimes referred to as purchase cards, corporate procurement cards or simply procurement cards, are a great tool for organizations looking to get rid of small-dollar invoices in accounts payable. They also can serve to make the procurement process more efficient. However, if proper controls are not incorporated into the P-card program, payment problems can creep in.

There is one other huge advantage in using p-cards. For the most part, the card issuer is responsible for issuing 1099s for payments made on p-cards. This is a recent change to the US tax code and relieves the organization of filing that information. In the past, this was a huge stumbling block for US companies. It no longer should be a consideration. In fact, if you have a vendor who is balking at providing W-9 information and it accepts credit cards, considering paying them this way and eliminating the problem. In this chapter, best practices related to the following are discussed:

- Designing a Best Practice P-Card Program
- Setting Strong Internal Controls in Your P-card Program
- Increasing Usage of the P-card in Your Organization
- Setting Attractive Payment Terms
- Increasing Rebates based on Card Usage

The Issue: Design of the P-Card Program

An effective p-card program needs to be planned out very carefully. Although most people understand what a p-card is, not everyone realizes that the p-card program needs to be well thought out and the mechanics of how it will work spelled out to employees. Assuming that because your employees know how to use credit cards, they will know to use the p-card is likely to lead to big-time headaches. Because when it comes to procurement cards, there's a lot more to the process than simply handing a clerk in a store your card and saying "charge it." To achieve a best practice p-card operation, you need to lay a strong foundation at the beginning. And that means the program must be well designed.

Best Practice: Each organization with a p-card program needs a formal written policy that is shared with all affected parties. This means not only the people who have and use the cards, but also their admins who might do the necessary reporting. Do not leave out any details assuming your employees will know something. You will learn the hard way that there a few who don't have the same knowledge base.

Your policy should address:

- ✓ Who should have a card, based on job responsibilities not title
- ✓ When the card <u>must</u> be used
- ✓ Where the card can be used
- ✓ List of preferred suppliers, where applicable

- ✓ Specific instances where the card should NOT be used (if there are any)

- ✓ Transaction limits – both dollar wise and number per day (if any)

- ✓ Spending limits – daily, if any, and monthly

- ✓ Detailed procedural instructions for end-users including but not limited to: card activation, card training, reporting, handling of receipts, record retention, the approval process reporting, handling of lost or stolen cards, and consequences for misuse.

Of great importance is the use of a cardholder agreement, which details the end-user's responsibilities. It should also clearly spell out the consequences of misuse, including the fact that the employee may be fired if the misuse is deemed egregious or of a fraudulent nature. This agreement should be signed before the cardholder is given the card.

The cardholder should also be required to undergo training on proper use of the card, as well as his or her reporting responsibilities.

The policy should be updated periodically, ideally whenever a change is made or, at a minimum, once every year. These changes should be reflected in the policy and communicated to all affected employees. It can be published on the Internet or intranet site for easy access by all employees.

Almost Best Practice: It is a good idea to limit the payment vehicles for each vendor to one particular type. This prevents duplicate payments from occurring because, for example, one was made using a check and another using a p-card. While this works well in theory, in practice it is not smooth sailing and may not be possible. For example, a card-holder may need to purchase something that is over his or her monthly limit. Thus, in reality it will often be necessary to break the principle of one payment approach per vendor. However, wherever a p-card can be used, it should be.

Special Pointers for Accounts Payable: Occasionally, you will have employees who refuse to use the card. If they cannot be turned around, request the return of their card. It is not a good practice to have inactive cards lying around. Folks should either use them or return them.

Cards should be retrieved from departing employees. This includes those who left the company on their own to take new lucrative jobs as well as those who were terminated for poor performance. When the cards are returned, immediately cancel them with the bank. If HR does not notify the card administrator when employees leave, periodically run reports showing cards with no activity. Investigate all entries on the report to find out if they have left the company or are simply not using the card. Terminate the cards of those who are no longer employed by the company. Talk to those who are not using the card. Sometimes a little extra training is all that's needed to get the employee to use the card. If not, and they still refuse to use the card, terminate the card.

Worst Practices:

- ✓ Not getting cards back from departing employees
- ✓ Not regularly updating your p-card policy and procedures manual
- ✓ Not sharing the p-card policy with all affected employees

The Issue: Setting Strong Internal Controls in Your P-card Program

Handled properly, p-cards are one of the lowest risk payment vehicles any organization can use. If you follow the guidelines listed below, your potential for loss due to misuse or fraud will be minimal. This is important because one of the most frequent objections to p-card use is the concern that the cards will not be used properly and put the company at risk. In actuality, there has been little reported improper card use, and the risk objection can be easily overcome by ensuring that the proper controls are in place.

Best Practice: There are a number of best practices every organization should use to ensure strong internal controls in your p-card program. Let's take a look at a few.

✓ Establish card policies and procedures for all employees. When a procurement card program is begun, detailed guidelines and procedures should be provided to all affected employees, including the admins who may do the reporting for their bosses. They are often forgotten.

✓ Limit the dollar amount of each transaction for each employee. This amount will vary depending on the person's job needs. These limits can always be changed if it is determined that the original level was not high enough. They can also be adjusted seasonally, if that is required.

✓ Limit the dollar amount that can be spent each month by each employee. In addition to the dollar amount each employee can spend per transaction; it is also possible to set up a monthly constraint. This, too, can vary by employee and area of responsibility. This control device limits the amount of risk a company has with the card. In extreme examples, these can be set as low as $100.

✓ Use Merchant Category Code (MCC) blocks. Companies concerned that an employee will take the card and go shopping for a new flat screen TV or take a trip to Hawaii can use MCC block. By disallowing charges at certain MCC codes, a company mitigates this issue. Of course, this matter can be resolved by the dollar limits placed on the employee for each transaction and for each month.

✓ Make a monthly review of all charge card statements mandatory and require a supervisor's signature on each statement. This after-the-fact review will uncover any spending that might be slightly off base. It also assures management that the proper oversight is being given to all expenditures, and improper spending not otherwise detected won't turn up. And hopefully, it puts managers on notice that they are expected to closely review the expenditures made by their subordinates.

✓ Make everyone aware that from time to time senior management and more likely internal audit will come in and review the statements for the entire company or any one department or individual.

✓ Set guidelines for where the card can be used. This will guard against the card's being used inappropriately. You might also include MCC blocks where you don't want it used – EVER.

✓ Institute strong card cancellation procedures. This puts everyone on notice that the card can be revoked at any time the corporation sees fit. This is especially important in the instance of employee termination. Regardless of the cause, the AP manager will want the ability to immediately cancel the card when an employee leaves the organization.

Almost Best Practice: As a bare minimum control, dollar limits should be set on the cards given each employee. This information needs to be clearly communicated to the employees so there is no misunderstanding.

Special Pointers for Accounts Payable: No matter how hard you work to establish strong controls over the program, there will always be exceptions that don't fit into the big picture. Whenever those loopholes appear, work to adjust the procedures so the controls prevent misuse or inappropriate use.

There is also something to be aware of regarding MCC blocks. Many organizations rightly put blocks on casinos. You can certainly understand the rationale for that. However, occasionally you'll have an employee who is attending a conference that is held at a casino. If you've combined your travel and entertainment card and your p-card programs and have put an MCC block on for casinos, the employee who goes to check into the hotel at the casino is in for a nasty surprise when he or she presents their credit card. It will be rejected. This is easy enough to get around, assuming you know about it. Simply remove the block for that one employee for the period of time they are at the conference. As soon as the conference is over, slap the MCC block for casinos back on the card.

Worst Practice: Worst practices include:

✓ Having no controls built into the program,

✓ Allowing employees to use the card as they see fit,

✓ Not getting cards back from departing employees.

The Issue: Increasing Usage of the P-card in Your Organization

P-cards are attractive to companies for a number of reasons including the fact that they get small-dollar invoices out of the invoice process, ultimately making the accounts payable department more efficient. As rebates become more commonplace, even for mid-size programs, the drive to increase usage within the organization intensifies. But, this doesn't mean haphazardly putting all possible purchases on the card. Rather a more reasoned approach needs to be taken.

Best Practice: Whether you are looking to increase usage because you want a higher rebate or you are simply looking to get some of those low-dollar invoices out of your invoice processing cycle is irrelevant. The techniques are the same. A few savvy companies have realized they can also improve their cash flow by using p-cards. They simply wait until the end of the payment cycle and then instead of paying with a check or ACH, they call up and provide their credit card information.

Here are a few ways best practice organizations have increased p-card usage in their organizations.

- ✓ Make sure everyone who has a card is using it every place they should be.
- ✓ Mandate the use; don't give employees an option.
- ✓ Educate every cardholder about all the potential opportunities to use the p-card.
- ✓ Increase the number of merchants in the p-card program
- ✓ Look for new opportunities to use the card. This can include things like paying for subscriptions, office supplies, and so on.
- ✓ Offer cards to all employees who make frequent small-dollar purchases.
- ✓ Whenever an invoice comes in that could have been paid for with a p-card, sending it back to the approver asking it be paid for with the p-card.
- ✓ With management support, refuse to pay any invoice with a check for which a p-card could be used.
- ✓ Consider merging your travel card and your fuel card into your

p-card program.

Almost Best Practice: None.

Special Pointers for Accounts Payable: Before you take any of the more aggressive steps mentioned above, make sure management supports the initiative.

Worst Practice: Not growing your program intelligently.

The Issue: Setting Attractive Payment Terms

How the corporate p-card bill is paid can affect a company's bottom line. Just as companies routinely negotiate payment terms with other suppliers, they should also handle their p-card obligations similarly. If the program is effective, the bill is likely to be one of a company's larger obligations. But realize that getting longer payment terms could have some ramifications. You may earn fewer rebates because of your longer payment terms. This is an issue each organization has to decide for itself. They need to determine which is more important: longer payment terms or higher rebates?

Best Practice: Your corporate credit card bill is very different than your personal credit card bill, and not just because it is for a much larger amount of money. In most cases, without further action, payment on the corporate procurement card bill is expected within 7 days of receipt of the bill.

A number of companies have succeeded in getting these terms extended to 14 and even 21 days. If you are a net borrower, you may be able to reduce your borrowing expenses by getting the payment delayed a week or two each month. If you are a net investor you may be able to increase your investment returns. However, you'll need to weigh that against any potential reduction in rebates. This is especially true when short term investment rates are low.

Almost Best Practice: None.

Special Pointers for Accounts Payable: If the program is not large enough, the issuer may be reluctant to negotiate payment terms. If that happens, revisit the issue when the program expands. At lower levels it is unlikely that the issuer will be receptive to your overtures—both on this issue and on the matter of rebates.

Worst Practice: Paying the bill before the due date.

The Issue: Increasing Rebates based on Card Usage

Rebates have become a hot topic in the p-card world. Once only whispered about, they are now discussed openly. Companies that spend a significant amount of money on their p-cards have found that card issuers will compete for their business by offering rebates, based on the level of purchases. For organizations struggling with cash-flow issues or ravaged by several years of a business downturn, this is manna from heaven. What's more, you used to need a million dollars or more per month of spend on the card to qualify for the rebates. But, that figure has dropped drastically in recent years.

What companies do with their rebate money is interesting. Some use it to finance projects they could not get funding for through normal budget channels. Others return it to the departments making the purchases, on a pro-rata basis.

Best Practice: Negotiate for rebates with your card issuer. Clearly this is a matter that the cardholder's organization will have to bring up. For, the card issuer is not going to broach the topic. As indicated above, the level of purchases needed to qualify for a rebate has been dropping.

Rebates are generally quoted in basis points, with 100 basis points equaling 1 percent. At this level, a company spending one million per month (or $12 million per year) might expect a rebate in the neighborhood of 5 basis points or $5,000 per month, or $60,000 on an annual basis. As programs get larger, the number of basis points the card issuer is willing to rebate grows. As with the terms, this issue can be used as a negotiating point when establishing a new program with several issuers bidding for the business.

Almost Best Practice: Ask for rebates, but don't necessarily take the first offer. If the card issuer believes the business may go elsewhere, it may become more aggressive in its offer. At a minimum, ask at least once—even if you feel your volume doesn't justify a rebate now. Let the card issuer know what you are thinking and plant the seed so that down the road, when volume increases, the issuer is ready to give your company the rebate.

Special Pointers for Accounts Payable: This is definitely a case of "You don't ask you don't get." In order for the company to get a rebate, it must request one—ideally during the negotiation process when the account is being set up. If you have a program in place without a rebate feature and the business is significant, broach the topic. If the card issuer is not receptive, you might suggest (with senior management's backing) that you are considering putting the program out for bid.

If your program is of sufficient size that you have one or more professionals working on it, you might want to consider membership in the National Association of Purchasing Card Professionals (NAPCP). Even if you have one person spending half their time on this issue, membership is a worthy consideration. By attending their annual conference (or their webinars and/or regional meetings) you'll be able to keep up on the latest issues and best practices affecting your p-card program. This fine professional organization also runs a well-respected certification program for those who are making a career out of p-cards.

Worst Practice: Never asking for a rebate.

The Issue: Personal Purchases on Company Credit Cards

While at first glance, the practice of allowing personal charges on the company card may seem harmless and a nice thing to do for employees, it has other implications that may not be compatible with running an efficient and effective payment process.

With a company credit card, the company is responsible for paying the bill and on the hook for any purchases made on the card. When a card is used for both personal and business use, it creates an accounting headache for the staff responsible for reconciling card transactions. It thus makes the whole process less efficient, and hence more costly, than it should be.

There is the added concern that allowing personal purchases on the company card is a slippery slope. First, there is the issue of whether all personal purchases will be properly identified. It's not likely that someone will identify a business purchase as a personal purchase and reimburse the company for it. Honest mistakes happen and they can sometimes lead to purposeful mistakes, errors that some would consider fraud.

Best Practice: Mandate that the card be used for company purchases only. Specifically, indicate in the policy that the card is not to be used for personal purchases. Use of the card should be limited to corporate purchases.

Almost Best Practice: None

Special Pointer for Accounts Payable: If your organization does go down the road of allowing personal purchases on the company card, make sure purchases are reviewed closely, especially in those organizations where this happens often.

If your organization allows this practice, it is even more imperative that the card issuer be notified of employee terminations and these cards be canceled immediately. If you think getting repaid for personal purchases is difficult while the employee is still employed, it pales in comparison to the difficulty in getting repaid by an employee who was terminated in a situation the employee feels is unfair.

Worst Practice: Allowing personal purchases on the corporate card.

The Data Scientist

Chapter 8: Payment Strategy

As the business world gets more complex, so does the approach we take to our accounts payable function. While we still have the same problems we had years ago, we've also got a whole slew of new ones. New payment approaches, mainly the shift in the US to electronic payments means there are some new issues to be dealt with. This is not to say that the new payment approaches should not be undertaken. To the contrary, like any other new process, it needs to be implemented with the appropriate internal controls and studied to identify early on in the game any new or emerging issues. In this chapter, we take a look at best practices related to the following:

- Establishing an Overall Payment Strategy
- Paying Small-Dollar Invoices
- A Rush or Emergency Payment Policy
- Payments Made Outside Accounts Payable
- Basic Fraud Protection against ACH Fraud

The Issue: Establishing an Overall Payment Strategy

Most never give a moment's thought to an overall payment strategy, unless they are considering stretching payments. But, that is not what this section is about. Generally, we believe that unless there is a cash flow issue necessitating the stretching, the practice can cause more harm than good. Not only does it antagonize vendors but occasionally leads to duplicate payments. And a vendor who is enraged over late payments is unlikely to return a duplicate payment.

But we digress. What we want to discuss here is an overall payment strategy that every company paying bills with more than one payment vehicle (checks, p-card, ACH, wire transfer, etc.) should have. The goal is to pay each vendor in the most effective manner. Having an overall strategy is especially important to those organizations considering both an ACH program and a p-card program. It is also exceedingly important for those who want to greatly reduce the number of paper checks issued.

Some reading this may wonder why establishing a payment strategy was selected to be included in the list of best practices. As many companies are finally moving away from paper checks, it is critical that the move be done in an orchestrated systematic way that does not create problems or issues that are not addressed. After all, the goal is a more efficient payments system, not one that is less efficient and problem-ridden.

It should be noted that during the COVID crisis, some companies heavily reliant on paper checks, quickly came to learn just how much of a hassle they can be.

Best Practice: Carefully evaluate each vendor and decide how you'd like to pay them, eventually. Ideally the answer won't involve a paper check. Once you've got your game plan in place, systematically convert each to the ideal payment mechanism. This may sound simple, but it will take time as no conversion goes smoothly. Start with a few vendors and once you are comfortable converting, ramp up your plan.

Almost Best Practice: Converting vendors to other payment methodologies without having an overall goal of eliminating paper checks. Okay, realistically, we should probably say, almost eliminating paper checks.

Special Pointers for Accounts Payable: Readers without a p-card program are advised to take special care when converting away from paper. If there is any chance you will at some point in the future embrace a p-card program, be careful about converting vendors to ACH who might later be converted to p-card payments. If you convert them to ACH and they like receiving their payments in that manner, they are apt to be displeased if you switch them to p-cards. While the payment might arrive at the same time, they will have to pay the discount fee to their bank, netting something like 97% of what they were receiving in the ACH environment. This does not enhance vendor relations.

Worst Practice: Having no plan or not trying to move away from paper checks.

The Issue: Paying Small-Dollar Invoices

Most accounts payable departments have limited resources they can devote to the processing of invoices. It seems like there are always too many invoices for the number of processors available. This means that those large-dollar invoices that really do deserve extra scrutiny don't always get their fair share of attention because too much time is being spent just getting those small-dollar invoices processed.

But what if you could eliminate some of those small dollar invoices? That would leave more time to thoroughly review those bigger items that deserve more attention. Since you can't just not pay low-dollar invoices another solution is needed.

Best Practice: P-cards are an ideal solution to the low-dollar-invoice problem. By putting purchasing cards in the hands of your employees buying the small-dollar stuff that creates all the small-dollar invoices, you completely remove the problem. Now, unfortunately, not every vendor accepts credit cards so you won't completely eliminate the problem. But, through a judicious use of p-cards, you can make a serious dent in the problem freeing up your processors to spend their time reviewing the bigger items more closely.

Of course, should you take this approach, you'll want to employ the best practices discussed in chapter 7 and institute strong controls around the process. You'll also want to make sure your payment auditors include your p-card purchases when they look for duplicate payments.

Almost Best Practice: If you can't use a p-card or the vendor in question doesn't accept them, you still may have some options. If the vendor in question sends many small-dollar invoices consider paying from statements. While paying from statements is normally not a good practice, this might be the one exception. This should only be done after conferring with the vendor. If this approach is taken, the system should be adjusted so invoices from this vendor cannot be entered. Typically, this works for items like office supplies, overnight shipping and hiring of temp workers. This may be the only time when it is acceptable to pay from a statement. Under virtually all other circumstances it is considered a very bad practice.

Special Pointers for Accounts Payable: Be aware that some vendors will still send invoices even though they've been paid by credit card. They claim they can't suppress the printing of an invoice. Closely scrutinize invoices from these vendors for they will often contain a statement saying either nothing is owed or that the invoice was paid with a credit card. Unfortunately, more than occasionally these remarks are printed in rather small font size and these invoices get paid. Identify those vendors who make it a practice of still sending an invoice and put them on an ACT (always check thoroughly) list.

Don't rely on the vendor to return these duplicate payments. Most won't. You'll either have to find them yourself or hire a third party audit firm to identify and recover them. Either approach is costly.

Be very cautious about encouraging employees to pay for items themselves and then submit them on their expense reports. Invoices should NEVER be paid through the expense reimbursement process. This is a weak control, makes it difficult to identify duplicate payments, and opens the door to fraud with those few individuals who might be tempted to divert company funds to their own pockets.

Worst Practice: Not having any strategy and paying all low-dollar invoices by paper check.

The Issue: A Rush or Emergency Payment Policy

Rush checks are the bane of every accounts payable function. In an ideal world where everything operated as it was supposed to there would be no need for Rush checks, also referred to as ASAP checks. However, in the real world almost every business has those last-minute emergencies requiring an immediate payment. Hopefully, we will get to a point, where we can refer to Rush payments instead of Rush checks, but we are not there yet in the US. Many, many other countries are already there.

The last-minute emergencies are bad enough, if they are legitimate. Unfortunately, in many organizations these emergency crises are the result of a breakdown elsewhere in the organization. An invoice may have sat unapproved on an approver's desk for several weeks, a manager may have forgotten to sign up for a conference that's happening tomorrow or a myriad of other things. When this happens and payment must accompany the order or invoice, someone shows up in the accounts payable office asking for or demanding an off-cycle check.

This is extremely disruptive to the staff and if it happens more than occasionally can cause a real drop in the efficiency of the department. It creates problems for those using positive pay, may cause a duplicate payment and finally, Rush checks are more likely to be fraudulent than one produced during the normal check cycle.

Best Practice: Make it a goal to eliminate all Rush checks. While you may never reach this goal, most organizations can come pretty close. Here are some techniques that will get you to that goal:

- ✓ Convince management that they really are a bad idea. Use the facts discussed in this section along with some numbers demonstrating just how expensive a rush check actually is.

- ✓ Make it *really* difficult for someone to get a rush check. This could include requiring a sign-off from the CFO along with an explanation of why this payment could not wait for the regular check cycle. If the CFO is a believer in eliminating rush checks, this step alone may do the trick.

✓ Identify the causes for rush checks by keeping a log of who requests them and why. After you have a few weeks or months activity, you should be able to identify trends and culprits (both at your company and on the outside) and then fix the problem.

✓ Identify duplicate payments made with a rush or manual check. Bring this to the attention of everyone involved and management. There's nothing like seeing a duplicate payment of a large-dollar amount associated with rush checks to put an end to the practice.

✓ Insist on paying electronically instead of by check. When you do get a request for a rush check, insist on ACH payment. Hopefully you will convince the recipient to be paid electronically in the future eliminating them from future rush check pools.

Almost Best Practice: None. This is an issue that has no middle ground. While not as serious as saying you'll tolerate small-dollar fraud, allowing Rush checks for anything but the most serious emergency opens the door up for more. It's one of those cases where if you give them an inch, they'll take a mile.

Special Pointers for Accounts Payable: This is one of those issues where you don't win any friends. Sometimes a staffer might be tempted to break the rule for a friend in another department or a popular employee. But this will come back and haunt you. As soon as others figure out what's going on they will a) complain and demand equal treatment or b) have the favored employee bring all departmental requests for Rush checks.

Please note that a request for a rush payment is an ideal time to try and convert the vendor to ACH. In fact, some companies only make rush payments using ACH, refusing to issue Rush checks.

If a Rush request is made without backup, follow up afterwards to get the backup. If an invoice is involved don't forget to extinguish the purchase order and receiving documents associated with it. For if you don't and the invoice shows up in accounts payable, the odds of it being paid are quite high as there is no evidence that it has already been paid.

Worst Practice: Allowing Rush checks making no effort to minimize or eliminate them.

The Issue: Payments Made Outside Accounts Payable

Research by AP Now reveals that 80% of ACH payments are made by the accounts payable staff. This means that 20% are not made in accounts payable. On the face of it this may not seem like a big problem. But, if organizations aren't careful about this issue, they could have a huge problem on their hands.

The problem revolves around the controls used in accounts payable versus the ones used by other departments making payments. Consider the following questions.

- ✓ Are they employing the same tight internal controls and strong procedures used in accounts payable?

- ✓ Are they doing the 3-way match?

- ✓ Are they using rigid coding standards?

- ✓ Are they extinguishing the PO when the transaction is complete?

- ✓ Are they extinguishing the receiving document when the transaction is complete?

- ✓ Are they entering the invoice number correctly?

If they aren't and a second invoice shows up in accounts payable, it will be processed correctly and payment will be made. For if the PO and receiving documents are open, why shouldn't the processor make the payment? And, it is an unfortunate reality that vendors rarely return duplicate payments without some external encouragement. This means either having someone on staff look for duplicate payments or hiring a third-party auditor. Both are expensive options for a problem that could be eliminated through some simple training and processes.

Best Practice: In an ideal world we'd have all payments made in accounts payable to ensure uniformity in process and that proper controls and processes were used.

While this might be a recommended best practice, we want to go on record as stating we realize that if the organization is already having ACH payments made outside accounts payable, this is going to be a hard change to get approval for. We therefore expect most will have to rely on the Almost Best Practice approach.

Almost Best Practice: Probably a more realistic approach is to offer same training to the group making ACH payments as is given to the accounts payable staff. If you explain reasoning in a calm and non-confrontational manner, you are likely to get concurrence from the other department. This means you have to be something of a salesperson, explaining why the fine points accounts payable insists on are so important.

Be forewarned that this will not be an easy task. Even if you get the manager of the other department to agree and the staff does attend your training, the odds are high that they will sometimes forget some of your pointers, like extinguishing an open receiver.

Pointers for Accounts Payable: More than occasionally, folks outside accounts payable don't fully grasp what can go wrong when best practices aren't followed. And, they certainly don't think about the financial implications. If your organization is one where payments are made outside accounts payable and best practices are not taken seriously, you will simply need to wait for something to go wrong. This may seem terrible on the face of it, but it's the only way to make your point, the accounts payable version of "a picture's worth a thousand words."

When you find a problem (say a PO not extinguished) NICELY point it out. Even better, if an invoice shows up and is processed and you're able to identify it as one that was paid outside accounts payable, bring this to the attention of those making that ACH payment. If you have a payment audit done (and every organization should), see if they find duplicate payments as a result of proper procedures not being followed by the group making ACH payments. Share the documentation from the audit firm to make your point.

It is imperative that if you take this approach, you do so very tactfully avoiding pointing fingers as much as possible. Make your points as diplomatically as you can choking back your instinct to say what's really on your mind.

Worst Practice: Do nothing and hope for the best. It will rarely turn out well.

The Issue: Basic Fraud Protection against ACH Fraud

The first thing to understand about ACH fraud is that everyone is at risk. Some think that because they do not make electronic payments they are not at risk. Unfortunately, this is NOT true.

With the sudden onslaught of interest in ACH from both businesses and unfortunately crooks, a review of the basics of how ACH works is in order. For without a thorough understanding of how these payment vehicles work, it is difficult for an organization to protect itself. We cannot underestimate the importance of understanding this payment tool as both users and non-users are at risk for various types of fraud if they do not take the appropriate steps. And then of course, there is the added benefit of ACH payments being a more efficient way to address invoices.

An ACH credit is a payer-initiated transaction. The payer instructs its financial institution to electronically transmit the payment through the ACH/Federal Reserve network to the payee's bank account. Typically, the funds are available the day after the transaction takes place. This eliminates all delays associated with mail and processing float.

An ACH debit is a payee-initiated transaction. The payee instructs the payer's financial institution to electronically transmit the payment through the ACH/Federal Reserve network to the payee's bank account. Typically, the funds are available the day after the transaction takes place. These transactions are initiated using your bank transit and routing number and your bank account number. It is implied that you have given your consent but there is no formal verification process by the bank to ensure you have given your approval. There are new bank products just emerging that provide some protection against unauthorized debits.

Without a doubt, crooks have turned to the ACH to perpetrate some sophisticated frauds. These crimes are growing and no one is immune. The crooks involved are increasingly sophisticated and the funds they steal often unrecoverable. It is important that everyone involved with payments understand the time constraints associated with identifying fraudulent ACH transactions.

As consumers, readers have 60 days to notify their financial institutions of unauthorized ACH transactions in their personal accounts. These include both ACH debits against their accounts and unauthorized ACH credits initiated from their accounts. As indicated earlier, the crooks in this arena are very smart. However, and this is a big one, anyone other than a consumer has only 48 hours to notify their bank of an unauthorized transaction. We advise companies to think of this as a 24-hour notice as they may not see if the offending payment for 24 hours, if they only check bank balances once a day.

There is no way around this. Monthly bank reconciliations won't cut it. Identifying a fraudulent transaction 30 days after the fact is too late.

Best Practice: There are a number of steps every organization should take to avail itself of even the most basic type of protection. Here are a few basic steps every organization should take.

- ✓ Put ACH blocks on every account where you don't want ACH activity to be initiated from
- ✓ Set up a separate computer to be used for online banking and nothing else
- ✓ Institute a practice of doing daily bank reconciliations
- ✓ Put ACH filters on those accounts where you will allow limited ACH debit activity
- ✓ Educate yourself and your staff to the risk and keep updated on this issue and the products offered by banks to protect your accounts
- ✓ Realize that positive pay only protects against check fraud, not all types of payment fraud

Almost Best Practice: None

Special Pointers for Accounts Payable: If you identify an unauthorized transaction after the 24 hours have elapsed, don't think you have no recourse. Still notify the bank. While they cannot guarantee the return of all your money, they will try and recover it for you. Often, they are successful although sometimes they are only able to get part of the money back. Still, some is better than nothing. So, the minute you suspect an unauthorized transaction, get on the phone with your bank.

Also, if you put an ACH debit block on an account because you don't want to allow ACH debits, don't forget about it. Too often an organization puts the block on and then several years later enters into a favorable transaction that will permit a vendor to debit their account. When the first transaction hits, it is denied because of the block, leaving the vendor in a less-than-happy state of mind. Still, it is better for this to happen once than to leave yourself wide open. You can apologize and promise it won't happen again.

Worst Practice: Ignoring the issue hoping your organization won't become a target of these insidious thieves.

The Issue: The ACH Alternative to Wire Transfers

Wire transfers are expensive. It's that simple. However, they are frequently used to make last minute payments for a variety of reasons. But, before you make your next expensive wire transfer, ask yourself this question: When does this payment have to arrive?

Best Practice: If the payment is under $100,000 and domestic, ACH is a very viable (and cheaper) alternative. And while you may think the cost is minimal ($10-$50) when looking at one transaction, it can add up over time if you are doing several a day. ACH transactions for under $100,000 can settle same day, and over that level next day. Yes, there is a small charge for same day settlement, but it is significantly less than the cost of a wire.

Almost Best Practice: None

Special Pointer for Accounts Payable: ACH payments should also be considered if payments are being made by check, especially if an overnight delivery service or messenger is being used to deliver the payment. The cost of these services can be quite high. Again, don't look at the individual cost of one transaction but the total spent over the cost of a week or month.

Worst Practice: Continuing to use costly wires without investigating whether a less expensive alternative is practical.

Tech Support and the Procedures Manual

Chapter 9: Policy and Procedures Manual

Because many accounts payable departments have grown gradually or evolved as part of the accounting department, few have a written game plan. Instead, procedures are developed on an as-needed basis, in kind of a hodgepodge manner. Moreover, much of the knowledge about how things work and where information is located often resides with specific individuals. If those individuals get sick or accept another job, the company is left in a lurch.

Every accounts payable department should have a procedures manual, to serve not only as a guide in case of emergency, but also to provide managers with the necessary documentation to demonstrate to management the capabilities of the staff and the work they are handling. Without such a document, few understand the scope of information that is needed to run a successful department. This is especially important for those organizations subject to the strictures of the Sarbanes-Oxley Act.

The procedures manual can also be used to determine whether any processes can be eliminated. Needless to say, this document will not be the most interesting book ever written, but it is essential. As an added benefit, it will make the auditors happy. The manual should not only be prepared by those who are actually doing the day-to-day tasks, but it should also be updated regularly. Some choose to do this anytime a process is amended or added, whereas others do it annually. It is imperative that this be done. You'd be surprised to discover just how much processes change over the course of a year.

There is one other reason to have this manual and insist that everyone follow it. Left to their own devices, processors in accounts payable will gradually develop their own procedures. Without a careful and periodic review, each person will end up handling transactions differently. There is a word for this, and it is *chaos*. If one processor has an idea for an improved way of doing a particular task, the suggestion should be raised with the manager. If it is determined that the suggestion is superior to the methodology in use, everyone should change how they handle that particular task, and the policy and procedures manual should be updated to reflect this change. In this chapter we'll discuss:

- Use of the Manual
- Creating an Accounts Payable Policy and Procedures Manual
- Updating an Accounts Payable Policy and Procedures Manual
- Providing Access to the Accounts Payable Policy and Procedures Manual

Issue: Use of the Manual

The policy and procedures manual for any accounts payable function should be a document that is actively used in the department and in other places as well. If regularly updated and accurately reflecting processes used, it can be used in many ways. Let's see how best-practice accounts payable organizations use their policy and procedures manual.

Best Practice: A good policy and procedures manual—and by that we mean one that accurately reflects accounts payable practices in use—can be used:

✓ As a training guide for new employees

✓ As a reference guide for existing employees—especially

122

for those tasks that are completed infrequently

✓ As a reference for other departments affected by accounts payable policies.

We're not suggesting that you give everyone in the company the accounts payable policy and procedures manual. Let's be honest; few would read it. But you can cut parts of the policy into shorter one-page documents and share with those who need it. The best example of this practice would be to reproduce the cut-off schedule for checks. This can be given to those who submit invoices for payment so they know the schedule and know when an approved item has to be in accounts payable in order to have a check cut in the current production cycle.

Almost Best Practice: Using the manual only for some of the items listed above, not all of them. By doing this you are not getting full value out of the efforts put into producing the policy and procedures manual.

Special Pointers for Accounts Payable: Managers who want to teach their staff to be self-reliant should point them to the manual any time they ask a question whose answer can be found in the policy and procedures manual. Sure, it's faster for them if you just tell them the correct answer, but they need to rely on the manual. This will also make the manager who spends too much time answering staff questions more productive.

Worst Practice: Worst practices include:

✓ Not having a policy and procedures manual

✓ Creating a policy and procedures manual and not using it

✓ Creating a policy and procedures manual and not giving it to processors to use as a reference tool

Issue: Creating an Accounts Payable Policy and Procedures Manual

An effective policy and procedures manual should contain clear simple instructions and not much else. This is not the place for long missives on philosophy or corporate policy. This is simply a big how-to book. It is not a place to show off creative flourishes or flights of whimsy.

Best Practice: The following guidelines will help you produce a manual that can be used to run an effective and efficient accounts payable function.

- ✓ Begin with a bare bones outline listing the topics to be covered.

- ✓ Use your outline to create a Table of Contents, breaking information into appropriate sections.

- ✓ Keep your instructions short. Break longer procedures into a few short steps.

- ✓ Avoid run on sentences. Review what you've written and break long sentences into two or three shorter ones.

- ✓ Use lots of bulleted and/or numbered lists (i.e. Step 1, Step 2 etc.).

- ✓ Include examples wherever possible especially when the concepts are not crystal clear.

- ✓ If you include jargon or abbreviations, make sure they are spelled out. Better yet, avoid the jargon and abbreviations, if at all possible.

- ✓ Include footers that number your pages.

- ✓ As the next to last step, run spellcheck to find misspelled words. Be careful. As you are probably aware, spellcheck will sometimes try and change words it doesn't recognize to common words.

- ✓ As your last step, go through your document and put the relevant page numbers on your Table of Contents.

Almost Best Practice: Acquire another organization's policy and procedures manual and update it to reflect your actual procedures.

Special Pointers for Accounts Payable: Be aware that this is a lot more work than it would seem on the face of it. Every organization handles their accounts payable function differently. So, you cannot simply take someone else's manual, make a few minor adjustments and have a good policy and procedures manual.

Worst Practice: Worst practices include:

- ✓ Having the manual written without consulting those who are doing the actual work

- ✓ Not making sure that the practices in use conform to the manual

- ✓ Allowing shortcuts that are not documented in the manual

Issue Updating an Accounts Payable Policy and Procedures Manual

Policy and procedures manual have a lot in common with wills. We all know we should have one and should periodically update it, but few of us keep it updated once we *finally* get around to getting it done.

Even if you think you have policies and procedures exactly the way you like them, circumstances outside the control of the department may force a change. A move to a new accounting system, starting to use electronic payment alternatives, a demand by a key supplier, a physical move by a group within the organization, a new CFO, or any one of a thousand other things can cause the department to need to implement change.

The very best manuals are updated every time a change to the procedures is made. This is one of the benefits of posting the manual online instead of printing hard copies. Of course, this is probably not realistic in most organizations. At least once a year the manual should be reviewed and updated. This is also a good time to ensure that the procedures detailed in the manual are actually being followed in the department. You will be surprised to find how often they are not.

Best Practice: Policy should be updated whenever a change is made to the accounts payable processes. Additionally, once a year, review the policy and procedures manual to not only ensure that updates were all included but also to see if any new best practices should be introduced to your processes. Use the following steps to complete the task:

✓ Find your old policy and procedures manual and dust if off.

✓ Review the manual and mark off all processes that have changed.

✓ Make a note of new processes that need to be added.

✓ Either assign one person to make all the changes or better yet, assign different sections to different staff members. Ideally the assignments should match their responsibilities.

✓ Set a deadline when the draft material is due back. Make sure everyone is aware of the deadline.

✓ A week before your deadline, send a reminder e-mail to everyone working on the project.

✓ Two days before your deadline, send another reminder e-mail.

✓ Collect all sections and review. If you disagree with anything written, discuss it with the author.

✓ Have all changes reviewed. Do this by giving each section to someone other than the person who wrote it.

✓ Resolve any discrepancies.

✓ Verify that what is written in the manual is actually how the work is being processed in your department.

✓ Publish and publicize. If at all possible, the manual should be put on your company Intranet site with access given to any employee who might need it. Highlight your check production and cut-off schedules.

✓ Thank everyone who was involved.

✓ Every six or twelve months, repeat the process.

Almost Best Practice: Updating the policy either once a year or whenever a new process is introduced, but not both.

Special Pointers for Accounts Payable: Be aware that waiting more than a year is really not recommended and waiting this long just makes the process all the more onerous.

Worst Practice: Never updating the policy and procedures manual

Issue: Providing Access to the Accounts Payable Policy and Procedures Manual

Producing a policy and procedures manual for accounts payable is important. But, if once the manual is produced, it is not shared with everyone who might benefit from it, you are certainly not getting full value for your efforts. More than occasionally, the manual is given to the accounts payable manager and that's it. While there might have been some rationale for this action when we had to print documents, it no longer makes sense. PDFs cost nothing to produce and the organization's Intranet site can host the manual for a minimal cost, if that. There's a lot more that can and should be done with the manual.

Best Practice: Obviously, the manager of the department should get a copy of the manual. So, should every person who works in accounts payable as well as the management team that supervises accounts payable. Finally, any procedure that involves another department should be cut out and pasted into a separate document and shared with that department. That way, they will know what is expected.

Some organization's print copies of their check cut-off schedule and then give a copy to anyone who requests a Rush check, so they'll know the deadlines in the future. This can also be handled through e-mail.

Almost Best Practice: None. Providing access to everyone is important; there are no half-way steps.

Special Pointers for Accounts Payable: When sharing the manual and parts of the manual, don't forget the admins who often handle payment related tasks for their bosses. It is probably more important that they get the information than their supervisors, as they are the ones doing the work. Don't horde the information in your manual. It should be readily shared with anyone who might have a need to see it.

Worst Practice: Worst practices include:

- ✓ Limiting access to the manager and supervisors
- ✓ Not giving a copy to every processor

✓ Not giving copies to employees outside accounts payable who are affected by the policies and procedures laid out in the manual

Issues with the Petty Cash Box

Chapter 10: Operational Aspects

There are a number of tasks that accounts payable has to take on that do little or nothing to adding value but still must be done. In this chapter we take a look at a few of those tasks that relate to the operational aspects of accounts payable. They are:

- Paying When the Original Invoice Is Missing
- Limiting Calls to Accounts Payable
- Petty Cash
- Reviewing Supplier Statements
- Adopting a Policy of Never Returning Checks to Requisitioners

The Issue: Paying When the Original Invoice Is Missing

Inevitably, no matter how good your processes are, an invoice will not arrive in accounts payable for payment. It may be lost in the postal mail, lost on an approver's desk or lost in intercompany mail. Getting a replacement to process and pay can be tricky, if you don't want to make duplicate payments. And, we're going to go out on a limb here, and assume that since you are reading this book, you don't wish to make duplicate payments.

It used to be considered a best practice to never pay from a copy. That's when it was relatively easy to identify a copy just by looking at it. It was before the use of PDFs and electronic invoicing became common place. Today, with a PDF copy of an invoice, you can have 100 copies of the same invoice and each one looks just as good as the next, making it impossible to determine which is the original and which is the copy. Hence this practice no longer works. Truth be told, this has become less of an issue because it is so difficult to tell a copy from the original. So often, a second invoice is simply submitted and no one realizes it isn't the original.

Unfortunately, when a copy or second invoice is sent, very few vendors actually mark the document as "COPY" or "Second Invoice." This has become a huge issue given the proliferation of duplicate copies of invoices that are emailed. Thus, it is imperative that the staff be able to use other tactics to identify a duplicate invoice. But occasionally an invoice is truly lost and a copy is needed.

Best Practice: Assuming that you realize the invoice being submitted is a copy or a duplicate, take the following steps;

- ✓ Go through the normal three-way match
- ✓ If that works, check the vendor's account to make sure no payments were made for the exact same amount
- ✓ If payment is being made on a check request form, go through the three-way match and make sure the PO and receiving document are extinguished.
- ✓ If it is a duplicate emailed copy, contact the vendor and ask them to stop sending duplicates. This will only work with some vendors, for a variety of reasons.

Almost Best Practice: None.

Special Pointers for Accounts Payable: As we move into an age where an increasing number of invoices are e-mailed or delivered electronically, this will be less of an issue. However, what will become a bigger issue is the matter of identifying duplicate invoices that should not be paid.

This also means that whenever an invoice shows up in accounts payable for payment greatly past the due date, it is incumbent on the staff that some extra checking be done to verify that this invoice has not already been paid. It could have been processed as a Rush payment, in which case normal best practices may not have been followed.

Worst Practice: Making no special arrangements to pay when the original invoice is lost.

The Issue: Limiting Calls to Accounts Payable

Very few tasks waste more time and adds less value than responding to vendor inquiries. Sometimes the vendors call themselves; other times, the purchasing professional who works with them calls. Yet, they must be handled and addressed in a timely manner. The issue is how to address this need without using valuable resources that could be diverted to more value add tasks.

Best Practice: The very best way to address this issue is to make available an online payment status portal giving vendors the opportunity to check their payment status online, whenever they want. In the very best online portals, they can check:

✓ Date payment was made

✓ Date payment is scheduled to be made

✓ If invoice has been received

In an ideal situation, these portals or as part of an e-invoicing system, an online dispute resolution module is included. This allows both sides of the transaction to communicate without ever having to pick up the phone. It also provides an electronic audit trail, so if one party is failing to communicate; it is readily apparent to anyone who checks.

Almost Best Practice: Assuming that an electronic solution is not available, try one or more of the following to get a handle on the onslaught of calls.

✓ Set a particular time when calls will be accepted, say Tuesdays and Thursdays between 1PM and 4PM

✓ Assign one-person to handle all calls

✓ Respond to all inquiries within 24-48 hours.

Special Pointers for Accounts Payable: One of the ways to avoid the calls is to anticipate calls and provide information so the call does not have to be made. This is especially true when it comes to providing data about deductions. Often, calls are from accounts receivable staff trying to apply cash. By making sure deduction information is sent along at the time of the payment, many of the calls can be avoided.

Some organizations chose to have each processor handle vendor calls related to the accounts they handle. The rationale for this decision is that they know the accounts best. And this is an important factor to take into consideration. However, if they are constantly interrupted with calls, their productivity will diminish. What's more, each person has their own set of skills. Handling disgruntled vendors is not something everyone is adept at. Better to hire one or two people skilled in dealing with difficult situations to handle the vendor calls and let the staff focus on what it does best: processing invoices.

Additionally, if payment is made on time the where's-my-money calls diminish in number greatly. While payment timing is usually not decided in accounts payable but at a higher level, the additional calls and how to address them should be taken into account when considering stretching vendor payments beyond the previously agreed to terms.

Worst Practice: Worst practices include:

✓ Not addressing the issue
✓ Not responding to inquiries in a timely manner necessitating a second call

The Issue: Petty Cash

Petty cash boxes have been with us for ages. The intent was to reimburse employees quickly for out-of-pocket expenses that could not be put through on expense reimbursement requests. The potential abuses of petty cash are huge. What's more, even where no malfeasance is intended, petty cash boxes are frequently out of balance, and rarely is there more money in the box than expected.

Petty cash boxes made sense when credit cards weren't common and corporate credits were not used by most organizations. That ship has sailed. There is really no good reason today to have petty cash boxes. Yet, anecdotal evidence suggests that about 25% of all companies still have them. For many it is a corporate culture issue.

Best Practice: Completely eliminate the petty cash box.

Almost Best Practice: Working to reduce the number of items and dollar level of items reimbursed through petty cash.

Special Pointers for Accounts Payable: You will notice if you glance below, that there are many more worst practices associated with petty cash than there are best and almost best practices. This is some sign of the problems the petty cash box can cause.

If there is a petty cash box, surprise audits should be part of the routine. What's more, like the master vendor file, access to the box should be severely limited. For if it isn't and there's a problem, there will be a lot of finger pointing and no way to determine who really is responsible for any losses. It goes without saying, that all transactions should be approved, reviewed and recorded in a log and the box should always be in balance,

Worst Practice: Worst petty cash boxes include:

- ✓ Allowing unlimited reimbursements in the petty cash box
- ✓ Not prohibiting reimbursing for items that should have been put through on an expense report
- ✓ Reimbursing for items that are expressly prohibited in the corporate travel policy

✓ Cashing personal checks in the petty cash box

✓ Accepting IOUs in the petty cash box

✓ Not limiting the number of people who can go into the box

✓ Not keeping the petty cash box locked and out of sight in a secure location

✓ Not establishing a set time each week to handle reimbursements

The Issue: Reviewing supplier statements

Some suppliers send statements because they want you to check them for any invoices you may not have received. Most accounts payable departments don't have the time to do that, although a few do. But there is a good reason to look at these statements. And that is to find any open credits you may have but don't know about.

The vendor may have sent a credit memo to purchasing or they may not have sent it at all. When the credit memo gets to purchasing, it is often filed or thrown away if the purchasing manager doesn't know what to do with it. Of course, many vendors never send credit memos so unless you take action, there's no way you'd know about them or use them.

There is one other dirty little corporate secret regarding vendor credit and supplier statements. Some vendors intentionally suppress open credits when they print statements to send to their customers. If you think this isn't true, ask yourself this. Does your accounting system have the ability to suppress credits when printing statements? Many do—and that functionality is in there for only one reason: end-users wanted it.

If you are wondering what happens to credits vendors never reveal to their customers, you're in for another surprise. In the past, sneaky vendors used to write those credits off to miscellaneous income. Unfortunately for them, when the state unclaimed property auditors show up, one of the first things they ask for is the miscellaneous income account and backup for all items. Open vendor credits are considered abandoned property by most states and as such, should be turned over to the state as part of the unclaimed property reporting.

Vendors who have no wish to do that have found another use for these open credits. They apply them to unearned early payment discounts, late fees (that you refuse to pay) and disputed items that you had no intention of paying. While some vendors who do this have good intentions and believe they are doing you a favor, others know exactly what they are doing.

Best Practice: Request vendor statements from all vendors at least quarterly. When the request is made, make sure the vendor understands you want statements showing all activity, not just outstanding invoices. Once you get those statements, review them closely and recover all open credits. You can do that by either applying the credits against new invoices or requesting the vendor cut you a check.

Some vendors will dig in their heels insisting you place a new order, if you want the credits. Don't fall for that trick. It's your money and you are entitled to it.

Almost Best Practice: None. This is money that comes right off your organization's bottom line. There is no half-way approach to this problem.

Special Pointers for Accounts Payable: Not everyone has the resources to continually check vendor statements. If you don't, hire an outside third party to do this for you. It should be noted that this is where most duplicate payment audit firms begin their recovery efforts, as these recoveries are viewed as low-hanging fruit. There's no reason to pay someone to get the easy stuff. Do it yourself and then call in the pros to find the more difficult duplicate and erroneous payments.

Worst Practice: Ignoring the vendor credit issue completely.

The Issue: Adopting a Policy of Never Returning Checks to Requisitioners

Returning checks to requisitioners is a royal nightmare for accounts payable. First, it introduces exception processing into the function. Someone has to identify the check that needs to be returned and then it has to be pulled from normal processing. And that is only the beginning of the disruption. Then a call or e-mail must be sent to the person requesting the return of the check to come and pick it up or it must be delivered. Sometimes an admin comes to get the item and other times the person making the request picks it up.

This is where the real fun starts. The check doesn't always get delivered. Sometimes it languishes on the execs desk, eventually getting buried under papers. Other times, the meeting at which the check was to be delivered is canceled and the check forgotten.

It doesn't really matter what the scenario, if the check isn't delivered, eventually the vendor will start looking for its money calling accounts payable. Again, this requires more of accounts payable resources to deal with the situation. None of these tasks adds any real value to the process.

And, we haven't even begun to address the fact that a few unscrupulous employees know that if they get their hands on a check, they can probably cash it and pocket the money themselves. And, that is precisely what a few employees do. There was one well-publicized case where an event planner for a well-known company used this approach to rip off her company for over $1 million, over the course of several years.

Best Practice: Never return check to requisitioners. This should be your company policy.

Almost Best Practice: If you can't enact a never-return-check-to-the-requisitioner policy, there are additional steps you can take to make sure that only a very few checks are returned and only under extreme circumstances. Develop a form that must accompany each request that the check must be returned. It should include:

    1) An explanation of why the check must be retuned

    2) The signature of a senior level executive

If the senior level executive is sympathetic to the plight of accounts payable and agrees that returning checks is not a good idea, requiring his or her signature is likely to dissuade all but the most diehards. And by having to explain in writing why the check must be returned will deter those with marginally acceptable excuses.

Special Pointers for Accounts Payable: This is an issue that has faded somewhat. In the past, the real excuse, although it was seldom voiced, was that the person requesting the return of the check wanted it returned so he or she would be asked out to lunch by the supplier accepting the check. This seems to be less the case in current times.

Often, requests that checks be returned to the person putting them in for payment are also Rush or ASAP checks. This is a double whammy and double cause for concern. If, as previously recommended, the rush payment is made electronically, the return issue disappears. If not, special care should be taken, including the form with the reason and the executive signature.

Worst Practice: Returning checks to anyone who asks.

The Issue: Printing Emailed Invoices

Unsurprisingly, email has overtaken postal mail as the method used by most companies to send invoices to their customers. There are cost-saving and productivity improvements for the vendor when they do this. However, 60% of the organizations receiving emailed invoices, print them before entering the data. This is NOT a productivity enhancement for them. A few need to have physical copies for regulatory reasons, but the majority do not.

Note: AP Now expects that over time the few regulatory issues will be eliminated.

Best Practice: Stop printing emailed invoices. This will greatly improve productivity. It's also good for the environment. Giving invoice processors two screens greatly enables the task of entering invoice data. The invoice can be on one screen for easy reference, while the data entry can be seen on the second screen.

Almost Best Practice: None

Special Pointer for Accounts Payable: Currently, only 27% of invoices are mailed. This number is likely to decrease to almost nothing over the next few years. A small investment in a second screen will quickly pay for itself in terms of cost of paper, cost of toner and improved productivity.

Worst Practice: Continuing to print invoices.

Why Coding Standards Matter

Chapter 11: Duplicate Payment Issues

It's a sad fact of corporate life, but many organizations regularly pay a very small percentage of their invoices more than once. An unfortunate part of the duplicate payment issue is the large number of companies that truly believe they never make a duplicate payment. While their processes may be first-class, mistakes happen. Additionally, fraud happens and the crooks who perpetrate invoice fraud know about duplicate payment checks – and they also know how to circumvent them.

In this chapter we'll discuss:

- Using Processing Standards
- Duplicate Payment Avoidance
- Mandating a Rigid Work Process or Eliminating Creativity when Processing Invoices Some Quick Checks
- Backup for Rush Checks/Payments

The Issue: Using Processing Standards

While most in accounts payable would like to believe that others are the cause for their mistakes, the reality is that sometimes mistakes are made in accounts payable, especially when each processor handles invoices in the manner they believe best. It's not that what one person is doing is wrong; it's just that unless everyone processes invoices in exactly the same manner, there are going to be duplicate payments introduced.

Best Practice: To ensure a best-practice accounts payable function:

✓ Establish detailed practices that each processor must use

✓ Develop a rigid coding standard to be used when entering data

✓ Periodically check your processors to make sure they are using the prescribed routines and not short cuts they've developed on their own

The coding standard should cover every possible permutation on data entry. Here are a few issues to be addressed:

✓ The way individual's names are entered (first name first or last name first)

✓ The way abbreviations are handled (IBM or I.B.M. or I B M)

✓ How to handle leading modifiers (The Gap or Gap)

✓ Use of full names or abbreviations (IBM or International Business Machine)

Don't forget to address industry specific issues, how to enter postal addresses, titles, and how to enter invoice numbers (do you include spaces, dashes, leading zeros etc.).

Almost Best Practice: There are no almost best practices. You either do this and are successful or you don't—in which case, you'd better be using a payment audit firm.

Special Pointers for Accounts Payable: If you take this step seriously and really set up rigid processes and rigid coding standards you will almost completely eliminate duplicate payments. It may seem like I'm harping on this issue. It's for a very good reason. This stuff pays off.

Worst Practice: Not establishing rigid processes and data entry coding conventions for the staff to use when processing invoices.

The Issue: Duplicate Payment Avoidance

The very best protection against duplicate payments is to make sure they don't happen in the first place. Now, if you're thinking "Duh – we know that" realize that not making them in the first place is not as easy as it sounds. What's more, some executives firmly believe their organization never makes a duplicate payment and alas, they are rarely correct. It's like the people who say they never make a mistake.

Best Practice: Best practices that help prevent duplicate payments in the first place include:

- ✓ Use of best practices and strong internal controls around the master vendor file
- ✓ Timely payment of the original invoice
- ✓ Use of rigid coding standards for data entry when processing invoices
- ✓ Reducing or eliminating all Rush checks
- ✓ Regularly cleansing the master vendor file of inactive and duplicate vendors

✓ Each time a duplicate payment is identified, review the paperwork to see if you can identify the root cause. Once that cause has been identified, work to eliminate the problem.

✓ Be very careful to check for the duplicate submission of invoices, especially from vendors who are known to send multiple copies.

Almost Best Practice: None; nipping the duplicate payment issue revolves largely on the use of rigid coding standards.

Special Pointers for Accounts Payable: Duplicate payments will happen, regardless of how tight the controls are. Accounts payable is often concerned that they will be unfairly blamed for any duplicate payments. Occasionally that happens. More often, it provides accounts payable with the ammunition needed to get the changes they want implemented. Too often, accounts payable knows that processes should be changed or improved but it cannot get the resources or support needed to implement those changes.

There is another untold tale related to duplicate payment audit firms. Some of them report that they go back to the same companies year after year, finding the same type of duplicate payments over and over again. It's not that the audit firm hasn't given recommendations for change – the company has just not implemented them.

Insist that the duplicate payment audit firm not only recover funds, but also identify procedural weak spots in your organization. The firms should also make recommendations as to what the company can do to tighten its policies and procedures. The recommendations from the audit firm are often the turning point that gets management moving.

Worst Practice: When it comes to preventing duplicate payments, some organizations are back in the dark ages. Worst practices include:

✓ Relying on the "memory" of the accounts payable associate to identify duplicate payments. This is an atrocious practice, unfair to the accounts payable associate, but is still used at some companies.

✓ Having no duplicate payment checks in your process.

✓ Not implementing any of the recommendations made by the duplicate payment audit firm.

✓ Not using an outside audit firm to check for duplicate payments.

The Issue: Mandating a Rigid Work Process or Eliminating Creativity when Processing Invoices

Standardization in the process is the key to avoiding payment problems in the accounts payable function. Without rigid standardization, a second invoice will be processed and paid should it show up in accounts payable. This necessitates the tedious and expensive task of identifying and recovering duplicate payments.

Managers who rigidly require their staff to rigidly adhere to a standardized process are occasionally accused of being control freaks. This is unfortunate for all they are doing is the best job possible at protecting their organization's assets. When it comes to processing invoices and other related tasks, creativity is to be actively discouraged. As we'll discuss, there is a way to incorporate new and better processes. It just has to be done in an organized manner.

Best Practice: Develop detailed standardized instructions for how an invoice is to be processed and how data is to be entered. This must include a rigid coding standard. These instructions and coding standards should be included in the accounts payable policy and procedures manual.

All processors should be trained using these standards. They should also be given their own copy of the accounts payable policy and procedures manual. Since this is frequently in the form of a PDF file, it isn't difficult or expensive.

Periodically check each processor's work to ensure they are using the approved standardized instructions.

Should a processor have a suggestion on how the work flow could be improved, they should be encouraged to share this with the manager. The manager can then evaluate the suggestion making sure that besides making the task at hand more efficient, it won't introduce any internal control weaknesses.

After the manager is certain that the suggestion will improve the accounts payable process without introducing internal control weaknesses into the system, an evaluation needs to be made of how the suggested change would impact other departments affected by the change. If they will be impacted, a discussion with them is called for to decide if they can work around the change or if it will cause them real problems.

Once everyone is in agreement that the recommended change is a good thing, it can be introduced to everyone handling the task in question. Everyone affected should be trained and begin using it on the agreed-upon date. Lastly, the accounts payable policy and procedures manual should be updated to reflect the change.

Almost Best Practice: None; this is another one of those all or nothing practices.

Special Pointers for Accounts Payable: By sticking to the rigid standardized procedures and using the mandated coding standard, most organizations are able to eliminate close to 100% of all duplicate payments. But this only works if everyone sticks to it allowing no exceptions.

Worst Practice: Worst practices include:

- ✓ Allowing processors to each handle their task as they think best
- ✓ Not having detailed standardized procedures for all to follow
- ✓ Not fully considering new recommendations
- ✓ Allowing processors to develop their own workarounds or shortcuts

The Issue: Some Quick Checks to Identify Duplicate Payments

Most organizations recognize that even with the most stringent controls and use of best practices, duplicate payments occasionally slip through. This can occur when:

✓ Invoices are emailed and snail mailed

✓ Invoices are emailed to multiple parties

✓ Invoices get lost in the mail

✓ Invoices sit on an approver's desk for weeks

✓ Companies decide to stretch terms and the supplier sends a second invoice because it did not get paid

✓ Rush or manual checks are used

✓ Fraud – both vendor and employee

✓ Disputes are not resolved in a timely manner
✓ A myriad of other factors.

Therefore, it is critical that they do some checking to ensure this doesn't happen.

Best Practice: As discussed above, use of standardized processes and rigid coding standards will help eliminate duplicate payments. Additionally,

✓ Identify the dollar level of what your organization considers a big invoice, say $100,000 or perhaps $25,000 and double check these larger payments to ensure that a duplicate payment is not being made.

✓ Create an ACT (always check thoroughly) list for vendors who tend to have duplicate payments more frequently than others. Routinely double check all transactions with that vendor. Similarly, if certain approvers tend to be associated with more duplicate payments, work with that approver.

✓ Review payments for identical payment amounts paid to different vendors.

✓ Using a payment audit firm to identify and recover duplicate and erroneous payments.

Almost Best Practice: Any other routine you can create that checks to make sure you haven't already paid the invoice in question.

Special Pointers for Accounts Payable:

The companies who believe they do not ever make duplicate payments are often reluctant to bring in a duplicate payment audit firm. This is false vanity. Since most of the duplicate payment audit firms work on an incentive basis, earning a percentage of what they find, bringing one in costs nothing. The other reason some companies object to duplicate payment audit firms is they think they are too expensive. With an audit firm, at least the company collects a percentage of the duplicate payment – without it, the company collects nothing. The real response to that claim is that it is more expensive not to use a payment audit firm.

Worst Practice: Doing nothing to identify and recover duplicate payments.

The Issue: Backup for Rush Checks/Payments

Rush checks, also referred to as emergency checks or ASAP checks, create headaches for accounts payable departments. They are those checks produced outside the normal check production cycle. They are supposed to be for those once-in-a-lifetime emergencies that crop up with varying frequency depending on the nature of the business and the tolerance of the corporation for this type of behavior.

In reality they are sometimes written to cover for the sloppy habits of certain employees. These may be executives who get behind in their work and neglect to approve invoices for payment, or harried purchasing managers who lose an invoice in the stacks of paper on their desk or the late-to-the-game employees who rushes in an expense report the day their credit card bill is due.

The problem with these transactions is that an employee in the accounts payable department is forced to stop his work to process the Rush request. What's more, payment audit firms report that there is an increased risk for a duplicate payment any time a check is written outside the normal cycle. The cost of recovering duplicate payments is huge.

There is one other consideration when it comes to Rush checks: the increased risk of check fraud—especially if they are also returned to the requisitioner. Finally, let's not forget that often the check issuance files given to the bank for positive pay sloppily updated. This means more calls from the bank on this issue.

These problems are compounded by the fact, that often the backup associated with Rush checks is slim to non-existent.

Best Practice: Insist on full documentation for every Rush request. This will enable the accounts payable staff to run the item through its standardized processes including the three-way match. If the back-up is missing, make the payment, if you must and then attempt to get it in the next few days. If you don't and the original invoice shows up, payment will in all likelihood be made.

Almost Best Practice: The harsh reality is that few companies can afford to take such a harsh stance. Nor are all senior management teams willing to back such a practice. Few accounts payable associates are willing to tell the secretary of the president of the company that a check will not be issued for the president, regardless of the reason. A more reasoned approach is to issue Rush payments without backup occasionally under very strict guidelines. Of course, try and get the backup at the time the payment is made. If it is not available, follow up later.

Special Pointers for Accounts Payable: While the accounts payable department is well aware of the problems associated with Rush checks, accounts payable managers also need to be aware of the corporate culture within their own organization. If the purchasing manager asks for a Rush check and accounts payable refuses, he is likely to go over their heads. If it imperative that accounts payable has a good read on how management will react. If 95 times out of 100, it will back the purchasing manager, then accounts payable managers are advised to avoid the confrontation, grit their teeth and find ways to work with purchasing to reduce the number of these incidents.

Worst Practice: Unfortunately, when it comes to rush or emergency payments there are many terrible practices being used today. They include, but are not limited to:

✓ Issuing manual checks whenever anyone asks

✓ Requiring little or no documentation proving that the Rush request has not already been honored

✓ Not checking for duplicate payments.

The Spreadsheet Guy

Chapter 12: Internal Controls

The backbone of any well-run accounts payable function is the incorporation of strong internal controls. Luckily, a good internal control structure goes hand-in-hand with best practices, so there is never any debate on that front. Without good internal controls, mistakes are more likely to occur and the door for an unscrupulous employee vendor or outright crook is opened just a little bit wider. In this chapter, we'll investigate the following issues:

- Appropriate Segregation of Duties
- Appropriate System Access
- Policy when Employees Leave
- Eliminating Weak Control Practices
- Staff Training

The Issue: Appropriate Segregation of Duties

Whenever the topic of internal controls is raised, inevitably the issue of appropriate segregation of duties is raised. It is sometimes called separation of duties. In government the related concept is that of checks and balances. It is the theory of having several people completing a task with no one person responsible for the entire operation.

When we talk about segregation of duties in accounts payable, we actually extend the concept to the entire procure-to-pay function (P2P). The idea is that no person can handle more than one leg in the P2P process. This makes collusion necessary to perpetrate certain frauds thereby making it harder for those few employees trying to play games and get money they are not entitled to.

Best Practice: The entire P2P function is analyzed and no employee has the ability to perform more than one leg of the transaction. Additionally, certain tasks provide the potential for collusion and should not be performed by the same person. For example, the employee that handles bank reconciliations should not also be responsible for unclaimed property.

Almost Best Practice: There are no almost best practices.

Special Pointers for Accounts Payable: Alas, this can be problematic in smaller departments as there are not enough employees to adequately incorporate a full segregation of duties. Under these circumstances there are two options as follows:

1) Most typically, certain tasks have to go elsewhere; or

2) Additional checks are built into the process to ensure there's no fraud.

The most common task that ends up leaving accounts payable is responsibility for the master vendor file. If the purchasing staff isn't sufficiently large enough either, then master vendor file sometimes ends up in another area in accounting. While it's nice to have it in accounts payable, that is not the critical issue.

What is key is that it is handled in a unit that can:

1) Provide the appropriate segregation of duties and

2) Will take the task seriously and handle it in a timely manner.

The other task that sometimes gets moved out of accounts payable is that thankless job of getting manual signature put on checks, if that is required. This is a task that most accounts payable departments are only too happy to have someone else take on.

Unclaimed property reporting, check printing, issuance of 1099s are other tasks that also get moved, if needed.

Regrettably, as long as everyone isn't 100% honest in the workplace, segregation of duties will be an issue all are forced to deal with on a regular basis. This could become a challenge as companies automate their accounts payable function, start making electronic payments in serious numbers and continue to implement process improvements that make the entire accounts payable function more efficient. These very positive actions will result in smaller more proficient staffs.

Worst Practice: Ignoring the segregation of duties issue completely.

The Issue: Appropriate System Access

This is an internal control issue that falls across all departments. But this work is only focused on accounts payable so that's where we'll direct our attention. Most organizations are pretty good about setting up each employee with the correct system access when they first are hired. But that's where many stop. After that they do a lousy job of handling appropriate system access. Many neglect to make any changes when a person is promoted or takes another position either inside or outside the company.

Consider the following, admittedly contrived, scenario. As you will be able to tell, it is constructed to make a point. Let's say you hire a new associate to process invoices. The person is given limited system access so all they can do is process invoices. This is how it should be. After some time an opening arises and you need someone to handle the printing of checks. The processor in question has done a good job for you so you promote her–and of course, give her system access needed to handle the printing of checks. After a year or two you have another opening. This time it's to handle the master vendor file. Again, the processor is promoted and given access to add new vendors or change information about existing vendors.

Can you see the problem? If each time the person in the example was promoted, the old system access was not cut off you could have a real internal control issue. You'd have someone who could set up a new vendor in the master vendor file, enter and process invoices, and print checks to pay the invoice. This would be a real breakdown in your internal controls.

Best Practice: The simple answer to this issue is to simply cut system access whenever someone leaves a position. This should be done regardless of whether they've left the organization or simply taken on different responsibilities, as in the example above. Often, this issue is never addressed and when it finally is after many years, the organization is horrified at what it finds. Hopefully, they don't discover this problem because an unscrupulous employee took advantage.

Almost Best Practice: Periodically run a report showing the system access for every single employee. Often, despite our best intentions, access isn't terminated when it should be.

Special Pointers for Accounts Payable: This task is often neglected when someone leaves the organization. The thinking is "what harm could they possibly do." The answer to that retort is "quite a bit." Just because an employee left under favorable circumstances doesn't mean that he or she isn't quietly harboring some resentment towards the organization. Don't take any chances. Terminate their access.

You know you have the problem if you ask someone who works for you to pull up information you should be getting from another department. This will happen when you've hired someone internally from another group. If he or she can get into other department's records, one of your former employees can probably access the accounts payable information.

Worst Practice: Not addressing this issue and taking it seriously.

The Issue: Policy when Employees Leave

When an employee leaves the company, he or she still has access to a number of things, unless steps are taken to cut those ties. Among other things, these can include:

✓ Access to the building, if the key and/or employee identification card have not been returned

✓ Access to the computer system, if it has not been terminated as discussed above

✓ Access to credit card sales, if the credit card has not been returned and canceled with the bank

✓ Access to potential expense reimbursement requests, if the employee has not been inactivated in the master vendor file

✓ Access to email, unless the account has been blocked or all messages automatically forwarded to a current employee

✓ The ability to sign a check, release a wire transfer, initiate or release an ACH payment on behalf of the organization

Best Practice: Whether HR's plate is already overflowing or not, they are the central repository for information about all employees. They are also typically involved with all employee separations, whether pleasant or remarkably unpleasant. This means that they are in the best position to notify everyone who needs to know about an employee departure.

As it relates to accounts payable, this means some departing employees have the access to do real financial harm to the organization, unless appropriate and timely action is taken. Therefore, it is critical that accounts payable be notified so they can inform the bank and terminate the financial privileges of the departing employee.

By notifying IT at the same time, the accounts payable function is protected, assuming IT cuts the associated system access.

Almost Best Practice: When HR doesn't notify accounts payable, there are some steps that can be taken to work around the issue. Some best practice organizations, concerned about tight internal controls, perform some of these tasks in addition to the best practices discussed above to ensure they are well protected. The additional procedures include:

✓ Periodically getting a list of inactive card-holders from the financial institution issuing the cards and investigating whether those on the list have left the organization or are simply not using their cards

✓ Periodically getting a list of active employees and running it against the list of cardholders and authorized signers to identify employees who have left

✓ Periodically running a report showing which employees have access to accounts payable functionalities and closing those that should not be in place

Special Pointers for Accounts Payable: Occasionally, management will be lulled into a false sense of security thinking that a departing employee was happy with the company and thus not taking proper steps. Don't fall into that trap. Don't underestimate the importance of taking care of what some think of as loose ends. They are anything but that.

Worst Practice: Not making arrangements to eliminate access when an employee has left the organization.

The Issue: Eliminating Weak Control Practices

Most organizations have a few weak control practices that can cause trouble. For many these practices have been around for years and no one has taken the time to identify and end them. In some cases this is because doing so will make management unpopular and in others, it's simply a matter of inertia.

Best Practice: Identify practices that introduce potential control weaknesses into your process and systematically eliminate them. These might include:

✓ Petty cash box

✓ Returning checks to the person who requested them

✓ Allowing more than the occasional true-emergency Rush check

✓ Not enforcing the T&E policy equitably across the board

✓ Not using positive pay

✓ Not having a payment audit

✓ Not mandating the use of a corporate T&E card

✓ Not cutting off systems access when an employee leaves a position

You can probably identify many more. From time to time you'll identify practices that do not provide the tight controls you want. Or you'll find weaknesses in your existing process, perhaps due to some other change. As soon as you find these items, work to eliminate the weaknesses and strengthen your controls.

Almost Best Practice: None.

Special Pointers for Accounts Payable: Accounts payable is in a state of flux and we expect that to continue for the foreseeable future. As new technology rolls into the workplace practices will change. As those changes are introduced, it is critical to ensure that along with the productivity savings afforded by the new technology, you do not allow weakened internal controls to find their way in, as well.

This means that whenever a process is changed, special attention is paid to the internal control aspects of the revised procedures. Expect to find weaknesses from time to time. This will require additional changes as you make sure the weakened controls are eliminated.

Worst Practice: Allowing practices that you know are weak to continue without looking for ways to eliminate them and/or tighten controls around them.

The Issue: Staff Training

Continuing professional education and staff training took a serious hit when the economy turned down. To be fair, it probably would not be right for a company to lay off a portion of its workforce while spending limited resources for others to attend seminars and/or conferences. But keeping up is more important than ever. Regulatory requirements are increasing, regulatory compliance is being scrutinized more than ever before, technology is making inroads and across the board, best practices are changing.

This means that in order to be effective, some resources will have to be devoted to professional development. In the past this expense was largely shouldered by the organization. In many cases it still is. As the economy begins to turn around, those organizations that cut their training budgets to the bone or eliminated them entirely are being urged to put those funds back in the budget.

Today, staff training also means keeping the entire staff updated on all the newest frauds and what is needed to protect against them. This has become critically important.

Best Practice: Make sure your employees have access to the latest information about all matters related to accounts payable including but not limited to:

- ✓ Best practices in accounts payable
- ✓ New technology
- ✓ New frauds and tactics to thwart those frauds
- ✓ Latest regulatory requirements (1099, unclaimed property, sales and use tax etc.)
- ✓ Customer/vendor relations
- ✓ IRS regulations related to expense reimbursements
- ✓ New regulations like the proposed corporate reporting (repealed before effective date) or Sarbanes-Oxley requirements (now effective)

This can be done by allocating budget for conferences, seminars or webinars. But, some of the technology requirements can be handled by attending some of the free vendor webinars. Professional associations, such as the Institute of Financial Operations, and fee-based newsletters, such as Accounts Payable Now & Tomorrow, also offer great information. And of course, there are a number of current books on accounts payable and accounts payable related topics.

Almost Best Practice: None. If the organization doesn't make a commitment to keeping its employees educated, the responsibility will fall to the employee. If that happens, some will rise to the occasion, but others won't.

Special Pointers for Accounts Payable: While it is recommended that staff training on generic accounts payable issues, such as those listed above, be obtained from outside sources, training about the organization's actual policy and procedures must be done in-house.

As suggested elsewhere, the accounts payable policy and procedures manual, if kept updated, is an excellent tool for educating new staff. Instructing of new staff isn't the only training that should go on in accounts payable. Any new process or change in procedures should also include training for everyone. And finally, periodically, the manager should review the work as the staff is performing it to see if any re-training might be required.

Worst Practice: Ignoring the staff training issue completely.

The Issue: ERP Access when There is a Change

Many companies have active programs to promote from within. This is a very good practice which helps improve morale and leads to a staff that is extremely knowledgeable about the organization and its operations. However, it must be done responsibly.

Best Practice: Close off ERP access when someone is promoted or leaves the organization. This way the organization preserves appropriate segregation of duties across the procure-to-pay process. Additionally, a report should be run once a year showing what access each employee has. This will help you catch any inadvertent failures in this regard.

Almost Best Practice: Some companies report they do this most of the time. While this is better than not doing it all, it is not good enough.

Special Pointer for Accounts Payable: This should be a no brainer but it isn't. According to the AP Now Practices Survey, just under 40% incorporate this practice into the procedures and follow it consistently.

Another 37% report they have the practice but it sometimes gets overlooked and about 15% don't address the issue leaving the organization wide open to segregation of duties mishaps and possibly even fraud. The remainder weren't sure. The practice is important not only for accounts payable, but for the entire company. It should be incorporated into the exit procedures and implemented 100% of the time.

If this step is not taken, the appropriate segregation of duties you worked so hard to create is for naught. One company who did not do this reported that when it ran the report showing who had access to what the first time, several long-term employees had access to over 50% of the ERP.

Worst Practice: Ignoring the issue.

The Issue: Who Should Receive Bank Statements

One of the ways, companies can uncover a fraud is by looking at the bank statement. If the person perpetrating the fraud is the person who receives the bank statements (and does the reconciliation) this very simple fraud detector is lost.

Best Practice: Bank statements should be received by someone other than the person handling the reconciliation or the person who authorizes or initiates payments. At smaller companies this can be a real issue. The person who receives that statement should open the envelope and, at a minimum, glance at it.

By doing this, they may be able to identify an egregious fraud. One company was defrauded of a good sum and did not notice it for several months as no one looked at the bank statements in that time period. They also did not verify information online, either.

Almost Best Practice: None

Special Pointer for Accounts Payable: Sometimes, in a small privately-owned business, the owner will have the bank statements sent to his or her home. This only works if they open the statements.

If they bring the statements unopened to work, as happens more than occasionally, the value of having the statements sent home is negated. This is because a devious crook will observe that the statements aren't opened and take advantage of that fact.

Worst Practice #1: Having the statements sent to the person who is doing the bank reconciliation, if that person has anything to do with the invoice processing or payment process. If they are completely separated from those tasks, the risk is lower.

Worst Practice #2: Having the statements sent to another party, who doesn't open the envelope to ensure no game playing is going on.

Cyber Fraud

Chapter 13: Fraud Prevention: General

Fraud is a sad fact of life, but one that everyone in the business world has to address. If they don't, crooks will take advantage. The term business world is meant to be inclusive of not only companies, but also colleges, universities, municipalities, not-for-profits, cities, states, associations and other groups.

While there are still the stupid crooks out there, most of our readers will find they are dealing with a sophisticated and smart bunch of people who know how to manipulate technology for their own gain (and your loss). Hence it is imperative that every organization take appropriate action to protect their bottom line. Criminals have become really good at finding new ways to defraud companies of all sizes.

What follows is a look at some of the best practices that will help protect your organization against the unscrupulous crooks trying to get their hands on your organization's money. They include:

- Separate Computer for Online Banking
- Wire Transfer Information Requests
- Information on Internet for Vendors
- Mandatory Vacation Policy
- Job Rotation Policy
- Handling Change of Bank Account Requests

The Issue: Separate Computer for Online Banking

The thieves involved in computer fraud are quite savvy. They are knowledgeable about how the banking system works as well as how to infiltrate your organization to get information that will allow them to take over your bank account. To do this, they find out who your employees are and what they do. With that, they can make an educated guess as to who does your online banking. Often, they are not quite sure so they'll focus on several possible employees within your organization.

Once they've figured out who to hit, they send a targeted e-mail to those individuals. The e-mail will look legitimate and their goal is to get the recipients to either click on the link or download the attachment. When the employee does that, a program is downloaded that enables the crook to capture the keystrokes made on the employee's computer.

With that information, they are eventually able to figure out where you bank and a good User ID and password. With that information, they initiate an account takeover and initiate electronic payments from your account. This is also referred to as a corporate account takeover. Individuals have 60 days to notify their bank of unauthorized transactions and get their funds back. Everyone else has 24 hours.

Best Practice: Obviously, the best way to stop this type of loss is to prevent the account takeover. Not using a computer to access bank accounts is one way but not realistic in this day and age. What is realistic is to set up a separate computer to be used for online banking only. It should not be used for accessing e-mails or surfing the web.

This inexpensive solution was first proposed by the FBI and the FDIC. Considering the cost of a stripped-down personal computer, it's really hard to understand why more organizations haven't adopted this simple best practice.

The best practice advice in this piece is meant to apply to both those who initiate the transactions as well as those who release or approve the transactions.

Almost Best Practice: None.

Special Pointers for Accounts Payable: Organizations that have adopted this practice need to make sure it extends to the person who releases the electronic payment transactions, both wires and ACH. Some busy executives have taken to releasing payments using their smartphones and/or personal tablets. While this by itself is not enough to cause a problem, many of these devices have not been outfitted with proper anti-virus software. What's more, even if they have, few update this protection as often as it should be.

If your organization has adopted this practice, make sure you don't inadvertently undermine it. Make sure the pc is turned off as soon as the banking activity is completed. This way no one will be tempted to use the pc when they're visiting the department. And under no circumstances should it be given to a temp to use because you have no other machine for them to use.

Worst Practice: Letting employees responsible for online banking activity use the same computer for banking activity as they do for downloading information from e-mails and clicking on questionable links.

The Issue: Wire Transfer Information Requests

This is an old problem that has persisted for many years. One of the pieces of information a crook needs to defraud your organization is your bank account number. This is especially true if the thief intends to produce phony checks. There are a number of ways to obtain this information but the easiest is to call up and ask for it. Clearly, if the crook calls and asks outright for the account number, they won't get the information they want.

Instead, they call up and say they are making a wire transfer to the company and ask for the wire instructions. Of course, when it looks like money is coming to the company; most employees willingly provide the information. That's part of the reason many companies don't make payments from the account that receives wire transfers. Funds from that account are swept each night into a general account.

Best Practice: Don't give wire information to anyone who calls on the phone or e-mails asking for it. Now if you are wondering what would happen if this were a legitimate request, you are not alone. Most will provide this but only to someone they already know at the company using a phone number, e-mail address or fax number they already have on hand. Otherwise, they could be giving information to a fraudster.

Almost Best Practice: None.

Special Pointers for Accounts Payable: This is another reason why getting good contact information from your suppliers and keeping it updated is so important.

Worst Practice: Giving account information to anyone who calls and asks for it on the phone or by e-mail.

The Issue: Information on Internet for Vendors

The Internet is a wonderful thing. It makes disseminating information to those who need it simple, cheap and effective. Unfortunately, crooks have figured out how to use the Internet to ferret information about companies they wish to target as potential victims for their antics.

Best Practice: In the absence of fraud concerns (see special pointers below) post information on your Internet site that will help your vendors in transacting business with you. If possible, set up a secure portal where a user ID and password are required to gain access. With this security in place, you can post all your forms, a blank W-9, and a Frequently Asked Questions (FAQ) focused on vendor issues.

If you routinely send out a New Vendor Welcome pack, it can be posed here as well. In fact, if you give new vendors access to this area, you can direct them to download the information rather than printing and mailing it. But take special care for unless this information is protected so only vendors can view it, you may find yourself dealing with crooks taking advantage of the information you've posted.

Almost Best Practice: None.

Special Pointers for Accounts Payable: Special care needs to be taken when posting information on the Internet. While you might want to make your suppliers aware of certain facts, say that you are paying by ACH, you don't want to share that information with those who could use it to your disadvantage.

Hence, unless you have a password protected site for your vendors, think twice about posting your forms online so they can easily download them. Unfortunately, they won't be the only ones downloading your forms.

Worst Practice: Posting all information without any concerns over who might view it. This is especially troublesome if you are moving to electronic payments and have posted your sign-up form, where fraudsters can access it as well as your vendors.

The Issue: Mandatory Vacation Policy

You may wonder why we are writing about vacation policy in a work that is devoted to accounts payable. While on one hand it is an HR issue, it also can be an internal control point. The theory behind making employees take their vacation time is that in their absence someone else would perform their jobs and if any ongoing fraud was in progress, it would be uncovered in that time frame.

Best Practice: Every person who has anything to do with the payment process (including invoice processors) should be required to take five (5) consecutive days off during which time someone else performs their job functions.

Almost Best Practice: None

Special Pointers for Accounts Payable: Under no circumstances should the person be permitted to perform their job function from home. This completely defeats the purpose of having the person take their vacation time. As an added bonus, you will develop backup for positions that previously had no one trained to fill in, in case of emergency.

It is worth mentioning that if the task involves use of a password and/or User ID, a new one should be issued to the person filling in for the vacationing employee. Otherwise, it will be next to impossible to tell who did what. What's more when the vacationing employee returns, the employee filling in could play havoc with your process and it would be impossible to tell who did what.

Worst Practice: Worst practices include:

- ✓ Allowing employees to never take vacation,
- ✓ Forbidding employees from taking too many consecutive days off, and
- ✓ Allowing employees to perform their jobs from home while on "vacation."

The Issue: Job Rotation Policy

There are many benefits to keeping the same person in the same job for an extended period of time. This is especially true when it comes to invoice processors. Not only does the employee get to know the job, but they get to know the vendors and the contacts at the vendors. This comes in handy when there is a dispute or a special favor is needed from the vendor. Unfortunately, there is a big downside.

This affability can come back to harm your organization when your employee gets too friendly with an employee at your vendor. If the two of them get close enough and decide to help themselves to money that doesn't belong to them, they can collude to defraud your organization and it will be a lot easier than if they didn't get along.

Best Practice: Wherever possible, rotate staff through different jobs on a very regular basis. If possible, processors should not stay with the same accounts for more than six months. This prevents the type of hanky-panky discussed above.

What's more, if they know they are to be rotated on a regular basis, they are less likely to try something funny; knowing someone else will be taking over the account and looking over their work.

Almost Best Practice: If you can't manage the staff rotations every six months, try every year or two. If someone leaves, take advantage of that turnover to move people around, perhaps under the guise of promotions.

Special Pointers for Accounts Payable: An additional benefit from regular job rotations is that you will end up with a well-trained staff that can fill in for one another in case of unexpected emergencies or absences.

You may get some resistance, especially the first time to try and implement a change, but stick to your guns. If you are having difficulty getting management agreement, your internal auditors will back you on this one.

Worst Practice: Allowing the staff to stay in the same position for years on end. This is especially poor if you also do not mandate vacations for the staff, as discussed earlier.

The Issue: Handling Change of Bank Account Requests

Most experts recommend that organizations pay as many vendors as possible using electronic payments, often referred to as ACH payments. And finally, the corporate world in the US is following. Of course, most companies in other parts of the world have been paying their vendors this way for a long time. But that's another story. With this change come a few new issues. One of those is a variant on an old fraud. In the check world, from time to time, companies had to deal with fraudulent requests for changes in the remit-to address.

The electronic version, with its own unique twists, is fraudulent requests for changes to bank accounts used for payments.

Organizations change bank accounts all the time for a variety of reasons. Many times, the old account is closed. Sometimes the company has changed its legal structure, sometimes it has changed banks. Occasionally, a fraud has occurred necessitating the change of account. Whatever the reason, when the change is made, if the organization has been receiving payments electronically, they notify their customers of their new account. Most often, notification of this change comes in the form of an e-mail.

Unfortunately, crooks, often quite sophisticated in the use of the Internet, realize this is a potential gold mine. They spend a bit of time analyzing potential targets and creating quite legitimate looking e-mails. These emails purport to come from the vendor, notify customers of a change in the account where payments are being sent.

As you might expect, the new bank account is one they control. Once money is sent to the account, it is quickly transferred out of the country making recovery difficult. Regrettably, if your company falls victim to such an e-mail it will still be on the hook for the payment.

Don't be fooled because the e-mail either looks legitimate or looks like it came from the vendor's e-mail account. Really smart IT folks can make the message look like it originated at the vendor's ISP.

Best Practice: An emerging practice that completely takes the onus off the customer is the use of automated self-service vendor portals, where the vendor is responsible for inputting its data, including bank account information for electronic payments and any changes to that information. This removes the onus from the customers.

However, as this is being written, most organizations do not have such a portal and therefore it is imperative that they do an independent verification of the request. This means contacting the vendor using information already on file to verify the change was a legitimate request. This also means regularly updating vendor contact information, something few companies do at this time.

It should also be noted that there has been pushback from the vendor community from using these portals. This means it is more important than ever that every single request be verified using contact information already on hand.

Some companies have taken this verification process one step further. They require employees to get online, find the vendor's website, obtain the general number, call it and ask to be transferred to the correct party. Yes, this is a lot of work and takes extra time. When you compare that with a loss of a significant amount of money due to a transfer to the incorrect party, the amount of work involved does not seem so bad.

Almost Best Practice: A few organizations now require that anyone requesting such a change not only supply the new bank account number but the old bank account number as well. This makes it much more difficult, but not impossible, for a crook to perpetrate this type of fraud. Some also ask for the last three invoice numbers or PO numbers or some other piece of information a crook is not likely to have.

Special Pointers for Accounts Payable: This type of fraud is expected to grow in the coming years. It is a variant on the change of remit-to address letters crooks sometimes send. Those too should be verified, again, using information you have on hand, not information included with the request.

Worst Practice: Just following the instructions in the e-mail or the letter without doing any verification that the request is legitimate. Equally bad is calling the phone number provided in the e-mail to verify the request. If it is a phony request the person who answers the phone at the number provided will verify it is legitimate, when of course it is not. This is why keeping current contact information is so important.

The Issue: Rush Wire Transfer Requests from High-Level Executives

Rush wire transfer requests from high-level executives delivered by email are just one of many of the 21st century fraud innovations on the part of criminals. They either takeover the executives email account, spoof the email address or purchase a URL that is very close to the corporate URL. They then use this fictitious email account to impersonate the executive and trick the lower-level employee into wiring funds.

Often these wires are for hundreds of thousands of dollars, if not more.

Best Practice: All wire transfer requests from CEO that arrive by email should be verified by phone. Crooks have gotten quite good at spoofing CEO (and other high-level execs) email addresses and doing it when they are difficult to contact. This is especially true if the request is marked Urgent or Rush.

Institute a policy of manual verification (yes, picking up the phone and calling) anytime an email is received purportedly from CEO, CFO or any other high-level executive with instructions to send money. While wires are the main methodology used, they are not the only ones.

Too often, employees who receive an email from a top-level executive are so intent on trying to impress the officer; they don't think to question the request.

Be especially suspicious if the request comes while the executive in question is on vacation and cannot be reached. Crooks are pretty good at ferreting out this information and using it to their advantage.

Almost Best Practice: None

Special Pointer for Accounts Payable: Educate everyone within your organization about this fraud. This means all employees starting with the CEO right down to the folks who work in the mail room. While that might seem a little like overkill, it is only a very little bit and you can't be too careful.

Provide additional education of the mechanics of this fraud to anyone involved with the payment process. It is critical that they understand just how easy it is to be duped.

Worst Practice: Assuming the email request is legitimate and doing the wire transfer without further verification or confirmation.

The Issue: Requests for Sensitive Employee Information from High-Level Executives

This was the next electronic fraud in the evolution of new frauds using phony emails. The Form W-2 scam has emerged as one of the most dangerous phishing emails in the tax community. During the last two tax seasons, cybercriminals tricked payroll personnel or people with access to payroll information into disclosing sensitive information for entire workforces.

The scam affected all types of employers, from small and large businesses to public schools and universities, hospitals, tribal governments and charities.

Here's how the scam works: Cybercriminals do their homework, identifying chief operating officers, school executives or others in positions of authority. Using a technique known as business email compromise (BEC) or business email spoofing (BES), fraudsters posing as executives send emails to payroll personnel requesting copies of Forms W-2 for all employees.

The Form W-2 contains the employee's name, address, Social Security number, income and withholdings. Criminals use that information to file fraudulent tax returns, or they post it for sale on the Dark Net.

The initial email may be a friendly, "hi, are you working today" exchange before the fraudster asks for all Form W-2 information. In several reported cases, after the fraudsters acquired the workforce information, they immediately followed that up with a request for a wire transfer.

Best Practice: Never release this information without getting a verbal confirmation from the executive involved that the request actually did come from them. For the most part, if you simply take a step back and ask yourself, "why would they want this information?" you'll realize that the request is fraudulent. W-2s are the last thing most CEOs would be interested in.

Almost Best Practice: None.

Special Pointer for Accounts Payable: Make sure everyone on staff is educated about this fraud and knows not to send information without further research and confirmation.

Worst Practice: Automatically emailing the requested information without confirming its veracity.

The Issue: Educating Everyone in the Organization about New Frauds

One of the most disturbing features of fraud in recent times is the rapidity in which new frauds are created and spread. This means it is critical that everyone stay on top of new frauds. By being constantly on the lookout, you can alert your organization to new frauds so they don't get snared.

To do this effectively, everyone on staff much be educated, no matter how high they are in the organization or if they are just starting out. If we've learned one thing in the last few years, it's that crooked are very good at finding vulnerabilities (both in processes and people) and then taking advantage of them.

One savvy reader of AP Now publications shared that whenever they see a new fraud, they immediately share the information with everyone on staff. This is a great strategy.

Best Practice: Update everyone about new frauds as soon as you learn about them. Many times, simply knowing what to look for is all that is required to prevent a fraud.

Almost Best Practice: None

Special Pointer for Accounts Payable: By simply knowing these frauds were going on, employees might have been able to recognize a fraudulent request when they received one. They also would have known not to jump just because the email looked like it came from a high-level executive.

It is no longer adequate to just take steps that worked in the past to protect your organization against all the different types of fraud that exist and are being created constantly. It is critical that everyone keep up.

Worst Practice: Limiting who information is shared with. One organization was victimized several times because they neglected to update new employees about new frauds on their first day.

The Issue: Quick Analysis: The 30-Second Smell Test

As just about everyone reading this is painfully aware, there have been a slew of new frauds over the last few years. A good number of them focus on mid and lower level employees. They take advantage of them, knowing they are eager to please senior management on those rare occasions when they have the opportunity. Or, they take advantage of a staff that is overworked and under deadline.

When you stop and analyze some of these frauds, it is pretty obvious that something is off. However, the criminal has impressed on the target that it is urgent that they complete whatever the task is quickly and without hesitation. And, too often they do.

Best Practice: With each out-of-the-ordinary request, ask yourself, "Does this make sense?" Often, if the target took just a few seconds to step back and ask themselves this question, it would be obvious to them that the request did not come from the part it purports to come from.

One savvy director of accounts payable remarks that she did not fall for the phony wire transfer request that was supposedly from their CFO because, "he never talks to me." She knows he would never bring the transaction directly to her and because of this has avoided falling for any of the numerous phony requests that come her way.

Likewise, with the phony requests for the W-2 files that have caused so much havoc in so many companies, if the recipient had just stepped back and thought for a moment. They would have immediately realized that there was no way their CEO would ever have anything to do with the W-9s.

Almost Best Practice: None.

Special Pointer for Accounts Payable: Keep in mind that criminals are very good at studying a variety of social media sites and compiling information. The fraudulent requests may come to the manager or anyone on staff. If the email says something like, "don't discuss this with anyone" that should be another danger signal. Make sure everyone on staff understands this … and take the few seconds to analyze the validity of the request before jumping into action.

Worst Practice: Not stopping for a few seconds to analyze the validity of the request.

The Issue: Sharing Information on the Company Website

The company website is a great place to share information with prospective customers, as well as vendors, both new and old. Alas, in recent years it has also become a treasure trove for crooks scooping out the origination looking for ways to defraud it.

The website is not usually an area that is thought of when considering accounts payable issues. However, the rampant development of new frauds now makes it a necessity.

Best Practice: Do not put anything on the website that might help a criminal defraud the organization. This includes, but is not limited to, vendor application, ACH payment form, change of banking details form, change of mailing address form etc. However, if you have a password protected part of your site for vendors, then this information might be posted there.

Almost Best Practice: None.

Special Pointer for Accounts Payable: Crooks are quite savvy. They are quite good at picking up bits of information on different social media sites. Employees should be cautioned about posting sensitive or personal information on Facebook, LinkedIn and other social media sites. This is not to say they shouldn't have a LinkedIn page. Today, everyone needs one.

But don't divulge information on these sites that crooks could use to facilitate a fraud.

Worst Practice: Posting any sort of sensitive information on the company website or any other easily accessible location.

The Paper Mountain

Chapter 14: Fraud Prevention: Checks

Check fraud, although it has been with us for a long time, still remains the most common type of attempted or actual payment fraud. Changes to the Uniform Commercial Code (UCC) have introduced the concepts of reasonable care and comparative culpability. Simply put, this means the person in the best position to prevent the crime will be held responsible.

Therefore, it is incumbent that all organizations take the appropriate steps to protect itself against check fraud. In this chapter we look at some basic tactics any organization should use including:

- Use of Positive Pay
- Pre-printed Check Stock Controls
- Check Stock Storage
- Other Check Fraud Prevention Practices

The Issue: Use of Positive Pay

Positive pay is the best protection any organization can use to protect itself against check fraud losses. It is a product offered by most banks that requires companies using the product to produce a tape that is sent to the bank each time there is a check run. The tape contains a list of check numbers and dollar amounts. As checks clear, the bank reviews the list before clearing the check to ensure the item is on the list. Once the check has been presented the item is removed from the list.

If an item is not on the list, the bank will either reject it or call the company, depending on the arrangements made when the product is set up. Those who issue frequent manual or Rush checks are advised to get the calls as these items sometimes don't end up on the positive pay file. Clearly, the company is advised to add them to the positive pay file when sending it to the bank but these items often occur between check runs resulting in a reporting delay.

It is important to keep in mind that check positive pay does not protect against all types of payment fraud, only check fraud. Many of the crooks who operate in the fraud world are very smart and very sophisticated with technology. Do not underestimate them.

Best Practice: Use payee name positive pay, if your bank offers the product. This is the latest development in an evolution of this fraud deterrent that has arisen as crooks find ways to manipulate the banking system. Once they understood the mechanics of the positive pay product, some of the smarter ones realized the only facet of the check that could be altered was the payee name. So, that is precisely what they did.

To counteract this new threat, banks developed the aforementioned payee name positive pay. Companies using that product also include the payee name on the file sent to the bank for matching before payment.

Almost Best Practice: For those using a bank that does not offer payee name positive pay, then the plain vanilla positive pay is the best choice. For those organizations that do not have the capability to produce a file for the bank, reverse positive pay is their best option.

Reverse positive pay requires the company to get online every day and verify the checks being presented for payment. If there is an item they wish to reject, they must notify the bank, usually by one o'clock. Whether no action means pay or not to pay depends upon the arrangement established with the bank. Use of reverse positive pay also means the company must have an employee verify transactions every day the bank is open, even if it is a vacation day for the company.

Special Pointers for Accounts Payable: Again, keep in mind that positive pay only protects against check fraud. Savvy criminals have figured out that they can represent positive pay rejects as ACH debits and still get their hands on your money. This is just one of the reasons that forward-thinking professionals realize that while positive pay is important in the fight against fraud, it is just one tool in an arsenal used to combat this insidious crime.

It should be noted that if you are verifying transactions every day using reverse positive pay, you are in effect doing a daily bank reconciliation. As you will see in other sections on fraud, daily bank reconciliations are now considered essential in the war against payment fraud.

Finally, positive pay exceptions should be handled by someone not involved in any other leg of the procure-to-pay function. For many organizations these calls from the bank are handled outside accounts payable. This ensures that if any hanky-panky is going on with someone involved in making payments, they don't have the "opportunity" to hide the problem, when the bank calls.

Worst Practice: Worst practices include:

✓ Not using any type of positive pay

✓ Not doing bank reconciliations on a very regular basis

✓ Ignoring the check fraud issue thinking it would never happen in your organization.

The Issue: Pre-printed Check Stock Controls

Check stock for paper checks has come a long way. A good portion of the corporate world has already stopped using pre-printed check stock. These are checks, preprinted with the company name, bank information and perhaps the corporate logo. However, they still remain in use by some reading this.

Those who rely on preprinted check stock need to do everything they can to make those checks difficult to forge. For this reason, safety features need to be incorporated into the check stock. Some of those features include:

✓ Watermarks. Watermarks are subtle designs of a logo or other image. Designed to foil copiers and scanners that operate by imaging at right angles (90 degrees), watermarks are viewed by holding a check at a 45-degree angle.

✓ Microprinting. A word or a phrase is printed on the check so small that to the eye it appears as a solid line. When magnified or viewed closely, the word or phrase will become apparent. Copiers and scanners can't reproduce at this level of detail, so microprinting when copied will appear as a solid line.

✓ Laid lines. Laid lines are unevenly spaced lines that appear on the back of a check and are part of the check paper. This design makes it difficult to cut and paste information such as payee name and dollar amount without detection.

✓ Reactive safety paper. This paper combats erasure and chemical alteration by "bleeding" when a forger tries to erase or chemically alter information on the check, leaving the check discolored.

✓ Special inks. These are highly reactive inks that discolor when they come into contact with erasure chemical solvents.

✓ Color prismatic printing. This type of printing creates a multicolor pantograph background that is extremely difficult to duplicate when using a color copier or scanner.

✓ Special borders. These borders on the check have intricate designs that, if copied, become distorted images.

✓ Warning bands. Warning bands describe the security features present on a check. These bands alert bank tellers or store clerks to inspect the check before accepting it. They may also act as a deterrent to criminals.

✓ Thermochromic inks. These are special, colored inks that are sensitive to human touch and, when activated, either change color or disappear.

✓ Toner grip. This is a special coating on the check paper that provides maximum adhesion of the MICR toner to the check paper. This helps prevent the alteration of payee or dollar amount by making erasure or removal of information more difficult.

Best Practice: Get rid of your pre-printed check stock by moving as much as possible to ACH (electronic payments) and p-cards. Clearly you will need good upfront controls to ensure your payments are appropriate and not duplicates.

For those items that cannot be paid with one of those two mechanisms, consider printing checks as needed on a laser printer. Obviously, you will need to build in the appropriate controls in the process and incorporate a facsimile printer that produces the check with a signature.

Almost Best Practice: If you use pre-printed check stock, it is recommended your check stock include at least three safety features. These make it difficult, although not always impossible, for a fraudster to copy your checks. More than three is certainly acceptable but if you want to be seen as exercising reasonable care, three is the minimum you need.

Special Pointers for Accounts Payable: Pre-printed check stock is fast going the way of the buggy whip, electronic calculators and VCRs. But as long as you are using it, it is imperative that it contain the requisite safety features.

Worst Practice: Purchasing the cheapest checks possible without regard to the incorporation of safety features. This makes it incredibly easy for the crook who manages to get hold of one of your checks. Replicating it is child's play and when those phony checks hit the bank, your organization won't be deemed as exercising reasonable care.

The Issue: Check Stock Storage

It's well known that banks rarely if ever verify the signature on a check. So, if your preprinted check stock is not held in a secure location, you could be increasing your chances of check fraud. For anyone getting their hands on one of your checks, could simply fill it out for whatever amount they chose, sign it and if your organization doesn't use positive pay, cash it. Even with positive pay, blank checks present a real and serious problem if they end up in the wrong hands.

Best Practice: Preprinted check stock should be stored in a secure location that is locked. Access to that location should be limited to one or two people. When setting up your workflow, keep the appropriate segregation of duties in mind when assigning responsibility for the check stock. Ideally it should be with someone who has no signing authority and does not process invoices. There should be no exceptions.

If the check stock is held in a storage closet, as it sometimes is, the key to that storage closet should not be given out randomly to anyone who might need to get something from the closet. That's why many organizations use a locked file cabinet in the locked storage closet to hold blank check stock. If they want to be really careful, the person who has the key to the locked file cabinet does not have a key to the storage closet.

Almost Best Practice: None

Special Pointers for Accounts Payable: Sometimes companies keep a spare checkbook around for Rush checks or unexpected employee separations. While they keep the rest of the check stock in a secure location, this checkbook might be kept in a manager's desk or a file cabinet in a highly trafficked area. Even if the file cabinet is locked, the key is often left in the top drawer of a nearby employee's desk. Unfortunately, this undoes a lot of the controls of storing the rest of the blank checks properly. Yes, it is much easier to have ready access to the checks for emergencies but it also introduces a level of risk that far outweighs the ease factor.

You should also keep a log showing how many checks were printed in each check run, the beginning check number and the ending check number. If you need any checks for alignment before printing, these need to be accounted for on the log as well. Finally, if any checks are damaged, they need to be accounted for in the log as well. The log should be periodically audited by a party not involved with the check production process.

The damaged checks should be kept in a folder. They should be marked VOID across the front if there is any chance they'd be useable and the signature block should be ripped or cut off.

Worst Practice: Worst practices include:

- ✓ Not locking check stock
- ✓ Ignoring segregation of duties issues
- ✓ Giving access to the closet where the check stock is stored to numerous employees

The Issue: Other Check Fraud Prevention Practices

Protecting the organization against check fraud is a multi-faceted job. Companies not only have to do everything they can to prevent the fraud from happening; they also need to sleuth out those instances when a fraud manages to get through their controls.

Best Practice: Other check fraud prevention best practices include:

- ✓ Don't return checks to requisitioners
- ✓ Ensure that vendor complaints and discrepancy reconcilements are directed to staff who are separate from the invoice processing staff

✓ Deliver checks to the mailroom at the end of the day

✓ Minimize, if not eliminate, all rush checks

✓ Establish appropriate procedures for uncashed checks to ensure proper reporting for unclaimed property

✓ Establish a separate account for refunds

✓ When an authorized check signer leaves the company, immediately notify the bank of the cessation of his/her signing authority.

Almost Best Practice: Implement as many of the best practices described above as possible. These should be integrated into your comprehensive fraud prevention routines.

Special Pointers for Accounts Payable: Sometimes despite your best efforts a fraudulent check slips through. One of the ways to get an overview of your organization (at no cost) is to hire a duplicate payment audit firm to recover any duplicate or erroneous payments your organization may have made. As part of that effort you should receive a comprehensive report identifying weak points in your process. Don't overlook this important report.

Finally, as we've mentioned several times already, many of the crooks involved in payment fraud are quite smart and knowledgeable about the banking community. They continually look for ways to circumvent controls. Unfortunately, they are often successful. When this happens the banking community often develops a new control or product to guard against the new fraud.

The only way for you to protect your organization on an ongoing basis is to keep up to date on the newest frauds and the products and strategies available to protect your organization. This should be an integral part of any professional's job, especially if they are involved in the payment arena. The best practice plan you put into effect to protect your organization today may need to be updated in six months or a year. So, don't rest when it comes to fraud prevention and detection. It's an ongoing battle – but one you can win, if you put in the necessary time and effort.

Worst Practice: Worst practices include:

- ✓ Using a rubber stamp to stamp on the signature
- ✓ Giving the rubber stamp to an admin to "sign" a pile of checks
- ✓ Signing blank checks and leaving them with an admin to handle emergencies

The Expense Report Tango

Chapter 15: Travel and Entertainment Policy

The travel and entertainment policy is any organization's first line of attack when it comes to getting its employees to conform to a set of rules of behavior and preventing fraud. In this chapter we delved into this issue in some depth focusing on the following:

- Formal Policy
- Expense Report Form
- Verifying Data
- Handling Receipts
- Detailed Meal Receipts

The Issue: A Formal Policy

The T&E policy should spell out the guidelines for company

184

employees when it comes to travel and entertainment. It details some or all of the following:

- ✓ What receipts are required
- ✓ What is allowable
- ✓ What is not allowable
- ✓ How documentation should be submitted
- ✓ What approvals are necessary
- ✓ Timing of reporting
- ✓ If cash advances are permitted and, if so, under what circumstances
- ✓ If corporate T&E cards must be used
- ✓ Reimbursement policy
- ✓ What hotel chains are preferred or required
- ✓ What airlines are preferred or required
- ✓ What car rental agencies are recommended or required
- ✓ Whether employees must stay over on a Saturday night if a lower fare can be obtained
- ✓ How unused tickets are to be handled

Best Practice: The organization's T&E policy should be formal, written, and distributed to all employees for easy reference. It should be updated periodically, no less frequently than once a year. Ideally, the update should take place every time a change is made.

Companies have eliminated all printing costs by publishing the T&E policy on the corporate intranet site or creating a PDF file. In this way, updates can be communicated quickly and the policy shared with everyone who might need access to it. Cost is simply not a consideration.

Whenever there is a major change to the T&E policy, a memo should go out from a senior executive explaining the change. The notice should be sent to all employees.

For a T&E policy to be effective, it has to be enforced across the board. This means that managers should not be allowed to override the policy, where they think it does not apply to their staff. Obviously, for the policy to be effective it also needs to be adhered to by executives at all levels.

Companies using an automated system can have a policy compliance feature built in. In these systems, reports that are in violation of the company policy are flagged for further investigation. The AP department can then return these reports to the approver's supervisor for further review.

Some of the more advanced automated systems take policy compliance one step further. They refuse to allow the submission of reports in violation of the policy. This is a bit extreme, as there will infrequently be occasions when an expense outside the policy is justified.

New employees should be given a copy of the T&E policy as part of their welcome packet.

Ideally, there should be a focal point for questions relating to the T&E policy.

Frequent T&E policy violators should be noted and their reports checked thoroughly each time one is submitted. (See the "Verifying Data" section later in this chapter.)

Senior management must support the policy in a very public way. Some companies do this effectively by having either the chief executive officer (CEO) or the chief financial officer (CFO) sign the cover memo that goes out with the policy. Others do it by having one of these senior officials sign a memo about T&E policy compliance that is put in the front of the T&E policy manual.

Almost Best Practices: None. There is no reason for a copy of the policy not to be given to every employee. Cost of production is no longer an issue.

Special Pointers for Accounts Payable: Processors should be given the right to question any item on any report, no matter how senior the executive whose expense report is under scrutiny.

Do not rely on the common sense of your employees. You will quickly find that you have a few whose idea of what is reasonable for business travel does not mesh with the corporate policy. In order to avoid unpleasant confrontations in this situation, make the policy as detailed as possible so there can be no misunderstanding.

No matter how good you are about educating employees about the T&E policy, via e-mail updates, memos, copies of the manual, and the Internet, calls will still come into AP about the policy. Additionally, violations will continue to appear on T&E reimbursement requests. A few flagrant violators will continue to claim "Nobody told me that," regardless of the vigilant efforts of the AP education team. The goal should be to wear these people down, forcing compliance through whatever means the company's policy allows. This can sometimes mean refusing to pay for flagrant policy violations—but only with very senior management–level support!

Worst Practice: Worst practices include:

- ✓ Uneven enforcement of the policy, which can lead to additional violations and higher costs
- ✓ Not having a detailed policy
- ✓ Not giving a copy of the manual to every employee

The Issue: Expense Report Form

There has been quite a bit of innovation and consolidation in the last few years in the area of expense reporting. Several of the companies providing third part services have merged. There has also been the emergence of SaaS (software-as-a-service) models, which effectively translate to a pay-as-you-go approach. And, of course there has been the emergence of Cloud technology, advanced mobile devices (both smartphones and tablets), and continued increased corporate scrutiny on expenses. Yet despite these advances, Excel spreadsheets still remain a key player in the expense reporting arena, especially where small and mid-sized companies are concerned.

Best Practices: Any automated form, whether it be created on a system purchased from a third party or developed in-house, can be e-mailed first for approvals and then to AP for submission. This makes the process much smoother and provides tracking information for those who want to know the status of their expense reports, reimbursements, and travel card payments.

If the form is automated, policy compliance can be incorporated in some of the more advanced systems. This is ideal, especially at a large company. It also takes the burden off the AP staff, who really should not have to monitor for policy compliance. By having the system flag policy violations, the company can take appropriate action with offending employees to bring them into compliance.

Reporting can also be done to aggregate where funds are being spent. This information can then be used to negotiate better rates with preferred suppliers.

It should be noted that when we talk about policy violations, we do not necessarily mean outrageous spending. A violation could be something as simple as not flying on the preferred carrier, not using the company travel agent, or not flying the cheapest route because it meant stopping over and losing an additional day's work time.

Some of the third-party models offer an interesting array of features. One that we like best is the incorporation of a link to the Internet that verifies miles driven, when an employee is asking for reimbursement for use of a personal vehicle. This software takes the addresses involved and calculates the actual mileage driven. We suspect this has put an end to some petty cheating that was probably going on in a few instances, where such verification was not available.

Almost Best Practice: If a third-party system is not used, at a minimum, the forms can be e-mailed for approval. The automated form should incorporate locked formulas. There is really no reason why employees should print out expense reports and attach his or her receipts before giving it to the supervisor for approval. If the supervisor wishes to see the receipts, they can ask for them or if they are scanned, automatically look at them online.

Special Pointers for Accounts Payable: There will always be employees who don't fill out their forms correctly, don't do the appropriate coding, don't do the math (or do it wrong), use old T&E forms, and so on. Each time this happens, take the opportunity to try and educate the offending employee.

Home-grown automated forms, typically developed using Excel spreadsheets, should have formulas embedded in the worksheets so the employee does not have to do the math. This eliminates the mathematical errors. The formulas can be locked, preventing the employee from tampering with the evidence. Some of these in-house–developed forms are advanced and work perfectly fine for even rather large midsize companies.

Worst Practice: Worst practices include:

- ✓ Use of paper forms
- ✓ Use of an Excel spreadsheet without locking formulas

The Issue: Verifying Data

There's a saying in T&E about "not spending a dollar to find a dime." It refers to the practice of checking every single T&E report in detail to ensure that no employee has charged something to the company that he or she is not entitled to. Some companies still feel the need to do this. This issue relates closely to corporate culture.

It should be noted that a move to a third-party automated expense reporting system (or an in-house model) can effectively check 100% of the transactions, without additional cost.

The problem of managers approving expense reports without ever looking to see what they are signing continues. The problem with this approach, as you probably realize, is that after a while the employee realizes the manager doesn't look and a few decide to push the envelope with what they submit for reimbursement. Occasionally it gets really out of hand.

Best Practices: Assuming you are not using a third-party system that automatically verifies each report, you will need to balance your verification requirements against the resources available to handle the task. Randomly selected expense reports should be checked in detail. The percentage of reports selected can range from 5 to 25 percent, depending on the corporate tolerances. Additionally, reports from the following should be reviewed completely each time they are submitted:

- ✓ Known offenders and rogue spenders
- ✓ Any report that contains a policy violation
- ✓ Any report over a certain high-dollar amount, say $10,000

This practice is referred to as spot checking.

Ideally, you will be scanning reports, so you can view this information online. If not, this will entail getting the receipts, if attached, or retrieving them if mailed in a separate envelope and verifying that all are included on the report.

Policy violations should be run by the submitter's supervisor for approval, even if the report is approved. Serious violations should be taken at least one level higher.

There is a growing practice of making managers responsible for the reports they approve. While a very few organizations have adopted a policy (and enforced it) of firing managers who approve a reimbursement request for something that is flagrantly out of compliance with the policy, most are not willing to go that far. However, a more measured approach is to make this lack of managerial oversight part of the annual review dinging the manger's annual increase if they have failed to properly monitor subordinate's expense reimbursement requests.

Almost Best Practices: In some organizations, there is corporate resistance to spot checking. Assuming the company in question has not gone to an automated system where they would get 100% review, there is a halfway approach. Companies that want to go the spot-checking route often start by verifying the data on half the reports, for example, and then working their way down to a lower level. This is a good way to start the process for those companies wanting to change the way they verify the data on the expense reports.

Special Pointers for Accounts Payable: Some organizations, especially those that want to set a tone of compliance from the top, will insist that all reports of all C-level executives be checked every time.

In theory, expense reports are reviewed by the submitter's supervisor and approved by this individual. The approver signs the report, indicating that he or she has checked everything and reimbursement is okay. The reality is that many supervisors don't review the reports and simply sign them without even glancing at them. This is especially true of higher-level executives as well as those in high-paying fields, such as traders, stockbrokers, and the like. Thus, sometimes checking reports is required and will not make AP popular with those whose reports are being checked.

Worst Practice: Not checking reports at all.

The Issue: Handling Receipts

When an employee completes an expense report, he or she must verify those expenses by providing receipts. The IRS guidelines require receipts for expenditures in excess of $75. Despite the fact that the IRS instituted this limit in 1995, very few companies have followed their lead. In fact, we are seeing a growing number of organizations now require all receipts. This is in stark contrast to the past when most organizations required receipts only when expenditures were in excess of $25.

The other issue regarding receipts is how they are sent to AP. A growing number of companies are now scanning receipts, even if they don't use a third-party automated expense reporting process.

Best Practices: There has been so much dialog around this issue and the growing practice seems to be that companies are now requiring all meal receipts as well as receipts over a certain dollar level for other expenditures.

When receipts are submitted to AP, they are either scanned or sent in specially coded envelopes. They should not be attached to the reports, from which they can easily become separated.

If receipts are scanned, employees should be required to hold onto the originals for 90 days. This gives the processor time to handle the report, spot check receipts and if they see something that doesn't look right, request the original receipt.

Periodically, even if nothing is wrong, the original receipt should be requested. This is to let the staff know the receipts are being reviewed and hopefully will serve as a deterrent to anyone thinking of playing games with their receipts.

Almost Best Practices: If receipts are not sent separately, get rid of those pesky little pieces of paper. Insist that they be taped to a larger piece of paper. Ideally, all will fit on one piece of paper. A company that sets the limit at which receipts must be submitted at either $25 or $75 should not have many little pieces of paper. Companies that set that limit at $5 can get tons of these little receipts submitted.

Of course, as credit cards continue to grow in popularity, there will be fewer questionable receipts. And, if corporate travel cards are used, this too will make a dent on the issue.

Special Pointers for Accounts Payable: Regardless of the dollar level set by the company, be aware that there will be employees who will insist on submitting receipts for every last cent they spend.

Worst Practices: Worst practices include:

- ✓ Verifying every receipt manually
- ✓ Not looking at any receipts

The Issue: Detailed Meal Receipts

Most restaurants, especially if you pay with a credit card, provide not only a receipt for your records but a detailed meal receipt. When submitting documentation for expense reimbursement purposes, the receipt showing the amount plus the tip is what was traditionally most commonly used.

However, a growing number of companies now require that the detailed meal receipt be turned in as well. From this the person reviewing the expense report can determine:

✓ If liquor was ordered when the policy prohibits reimbursement for liquor

✓ If an inappropriate amount of liquor was ordered

✓ How many adults were at the meal

✓ If kiddie meals were ordered

✓ If something (mainly gift cards) was paid for in addition to the meal

Unfortunately, there have been numerous instances where all of the above have been included in expense reimbursement requests. Without the detailed meal receipt, it is possible to mask the inappropriate purchases.

One would hope that if the detailed meal receipt is required, employees would be smart enough to avoid the types of behavior described above, as well as any other shenanigans they might dream up. Thus, requiring the detailed meal receipt serves more as a deterrent than a tool to actually find fraud—or at least, one would hope the requirement would deter that type of inappropriate spend.

Best Practice: Require but spot check meal receipts with expense reimbursement reports to verify policy compliance and non-inclusion of gift cards and other items not normally reimbursed on expense reports.

Almost Best Practice: None.

Special Pointers for Accounts Payable: Sometimes when someone hears about the requirement to get the detailed meal receipt for every meal, they start to question the appropriateness; given the extra work verifying those receipts is likely to create. The important issue is that not every meal receipt will be checked. For the most part, they are to be spot checked like other receipts. Of course, if you have your list of known expense reimbursement abusers, verify all their receipts, all the time.

Worst Practice: Allowing the expense to be documented by either the detailed receipt or the receipt showing the total payment. This opens the door for the receipt to be submitted twice, perhaps by two different employees.

The Issue: Use of a Personal Card

Many organizations, including those with a corporate card, allow employees to use their personal cards. Data from a recent AP Now survey reveals that this is the situation in almost half the organizations. The rationale is that the employee wants to get points or other benefits and it doesn't hurt the company. This thinking is wrong.

For starters, use of a personal card instead of a company card creates more work for the team administering expense reports. Unless the organization is willing to hire additional staff to handle that additional work, it is disingenuous to pretend it doesn't cost anything. In my experience, there are few companies willing to take on this extra expense.

Even more hurtful is the fact that use of a personal card facilitates fraud. Thinking that no one in your organization would play games with their expense reports is also not clear thinking. Overwhelmingly, the data shows otherwise.

Best Practice: Mandate the use of a company card for all travel and entertainment related expenses.

Almost Best Practice: None.

Special Pointer for Accounts Payable: When game playing with expense reporting and cards takes place, many organizations refer to it as policy or card abuse. But, at the end of the day, if the employee knowingly uses the card in a manner to gain reimbursement for something they are not entitled to get, that is fraud, to my way of thinking.

One way to encourage use of the company card, if management won't restrict the use of personal cards revolves around receipts. The IRS only requires receipts for expenditures $75 and higher. Consider adopting a policy of requiring all receipts if the personal card is used by only receipts over $75 if the company card is used. You won't convert all those employees who insist on using their personal cards, but you will get a large chunk of them over time.

Worst Practice: Allowing unfettered use of personal cards.

The Issue: Recovering Refunds on Personal Cards

Whenever a refund is made for a purchase made on a credit card, the refund is charged back to the card on which the purchase was made. This is regardless of what it was for or whether it is a personal or corporate card.

The problem arises when the purchase is made by an employee on their personal card for an item expensed on an expense report. Then the employee is expected to reimburse their employer. It is commonly acknowledged that more than occasionally, employees forget to reimburse their employer.

While this is always a problem, it was not a huge one until COVID hit. Then, with conferences and seminars being cancelled, almost across the board, it became a huge issue. Because, it was not only the fees for these events that were problematic, but also related airfares and sometimes hotel pre-payments.

Suddenly, companies weren't looking at one or two refunds a month, but many times that. In a few organizations, there were thousands of transactions to be tracked. The matter was complicated by the issue that some events were issuing refunds, while others provided the option of simply moving the event registration to the following year. Airlines too were trying to convince travelers to take a credit for future travel rather than a straight refund.

This issue can be completely avoided by NOT allowing employees to use personal cards when making business purchases. However, almost half of all companies still allow this questionable practice.

Best Practice: Require employee to reimburse company for refunds put through on personal cards immediately – not the next time they prepare an expense report. It's just too easy to forget it. Make this part of your Travel Policy and a regular procedure.

Almost Best Practice: None

Special Pointer for Accounts Payable: If and when you discover a refund was not turned back to the organization, you must treat it as an honest mistake. Even if you know in your heart it was not, do not accuse the person of dishonest behavior. For starters, you could be wrong. It's happened more than once. Plus, you will need to work with this person for the foreseeable future and you don't want those interactions to be any tenser than they have to be.

What you can do is make sure that individual's expense reports always get a thorough review. But do NOT tell them this, no matter how tempted you are.

Allowing employees to use personal cards when the organization has gone through the trouble and expense of getting a company card is NOT a best practice. Under the best of circumstances, it creates some extra work and facilitates certain types of petty fraud. These issues are all magnified post COVID.

Worst Practice: Not making an effort to check for refunds when employees are using personal cards.

The Issue: Reimbursements for Working from Home Expenses

Reimbursing for working from home expenses has not been a big issue in most companies. Few employees worked remotely and those that did often did so only on a part-time basis and as an accommodation by their employers. So, few worried about or had a policy for reimbursing remote working expenses.

Then COVID hit and all that changed. The expectation is that when things return to normal (whatever that may look like), a sizeable number of companies will have staff working from home either part of the time or full time. That changes the equation. When you go from a scenario where remote working is seen as an accommodation to employee to one where it is mandated, the expense issue takes on a whole different hue.

Thus, what one party thinks it's reasonable, the next finds completely unacceptable. Also, individuals have a wide variety of ideas as to what is reasonable when it comes to their companies paying for certain things.

Best Practice: Create a formal written policy that clearly delineates what a company will pay for and what it won't. If not exists, the sooner one is created and shared with employees the better. This policy should be created at the management level, by the same executives who create the travel policy.

Almost Best Practice: None.

Special Pointer for Accounts Payable: This is precisely the same as travel expense reimbursement request. If you are in the position to review expense reports then you know that sometimes people get a little crazy when it comes to what they put in for. Therefore, if your organization does not have a written policy, push for one. For the sooner you get one, the easier it will be to enforce.

Worst Practice: Not having a formal policy and allowing each department to do as it sees fit. This will result in an inequitable treatment of employees.

Why Detailed Meal Receipts Matter

Chapter 16: Expense Reporting Issues

Expense reporting has a lot of issues associated with it and all need to be addressed carefully or chaos will ensue. In this chapter we take a look at the best practices associated with:

- Cash Advances
- Unused Tickets
- Departing Employees
- Making Travel Reservations
- Reimbursing Employees

The Issue: Cash Advances

Before corporate credit cards were commonplace, employees would routinely pay for all their travel expenses themselves. Airline tickets had to be booked and paid for weeks, if not months, in advance. Upon completion of a trip, they would submit their expense report to obtain their reimbursement, as they do today. The difference was that traveling employees could be out of pocket for significant amounts of money, especially if they traveled frequently, to foreign countries, or first class.

Thus, the practice of cash advances evolved. To help the financially overburdened traveling executive, companies would advance them some amount of cash to cover these expenses. Upon the completion of the trip(s) and the expense report, the two would be reconciled and a settling up would occur. More often than not, this entailed the employee's writing a check for the amount he or she owed the company. If you are sitting there scratching your head, consider the following facts:

- ✓ There usually were no limits on the cash advance.

- ✓ There was no interest charged on the cash advance loan.

- ✓ Interest rates for the last 10- 30 years ago were high (or very high) compared with today's rates.

- ✓ Few employees are willing to pay out of pocket when their employers offer a no-cost alternative—the cash advance.

Clearly, not all employees abused the cash advance system. Nothing could be farther from the truth. However, some employees who have to return part of the advance frequently drag their feet in completing their expense reimbursement reports. This exacerbates the already problematic issue of getting all employees to complete their reports on time.

The other factor affecting cash advances is that, in a few cases, employees are tempted to fabricate expenses to justify not returning the cash.

Finally, there are the financial implications and procedural inefficiencies of the cash advance process. In higher-interest-rate environments, the lost interest income or the increased borrowing costs associated with cash advances were a factor. Even today, in a relatively low-interest-rate situation, there are cash flow implications. When cash advances are used, they have to be accounted for correctly and issued in the form of either cash or checks. Neither process adds value.

Best Practice: Don't give cash advances. Not every company is willing to take the "just say no to cash advances" stance. It may go against the corporate culture, or it may not be feasible given the level of employees who are asked to travel on the company's behalf. If advances are given, they should be only under special circumstances, with the approval of both the individual's direct supervisor and the supervisor's supervisor. Make it difficult, not impossible, so people will consider seriously before asking for an advance.

If a cash advance is provided, do it in the form of an electronic (ACH) payment. Giving cash advances in the form of cash is rife with procedural issues and can lead to abuses.

Special Pointers for Accounts Payable: Realize that if you have new employees just out of school who are required to travel, you may have to give them cash advances as they may not be able to fund the trips themselves. This is especially true if your organization does not offer its employees a company paid travel card.

Worst Practice: Worst practices include:

- ✓ Routinely giving cash advances
- ✓ Not following up with employees who receive cash advances to make sure expense reports are submitted on a timely basis
- ✓ Using cash for cash advances
- ✓ Not using a consistent policy for cash advances

The Issue: Unused Tickets

The plans of business travelers change frequently. The result is unused tickets. With paper tickets, at least travelers have the piece of cardboard to remind them that the ticket was not used and can be either exchanged for another ticket or refunded. With e-tickets, this reminder is not available. Since many business travelers now purchase nonrefundable tickets, they are then faced with a ticket that can be used only against future travel and not refunded. Thus, it is necessary to keep track of these tickets.

Even if the ticket can be refunded, it is necessary that someone take the necessary steps to get the refund. In the past, travel agents helped get these refunds. With few organizations relying on travel agents, the task now falls to the individual traveler or perhaps the admin within the department. If no action is taken, the ticket will expire (typically within one year) worthless.

This is an issue that should be considered when booking travel. Instead of automatically purchasing the cheapest ticket, some consideration should be given to whether the trip is likely to be canceled. If this is the case, consider buying a refundable ticket and paying the price. Sometimes, the price difference is small. This is especially important if the employee in question is not someone who travels frequently.

If you are dealing with unused tickets from travel planned to take place during the COVID crisis, make sure to refer to the section on Refunds.

Best Practice: A formal procedure should be put in place to handle unused tickets. American Express says that more than 4 percent of e-tickets issued by corporate travel departments go unused. New systems have emerged to track unused e-tickets and even process refunds; however, many companies are unaware of these systems.

If you use a third-party expense reporting system, talk to the service provider to see what options they have for tracking unused tickets. Make sure to activate that feature, if it is available.

Almost Best Practice: Have someone in the travel office or department track the status of unused tickets and send reminders to travelers who have them.

Special Pointers for Accounts Payable: Unused tickets will be an issue as long as company employees travel. Find some system to track them; otherwise, even the most conscientious travelers will forget about them.

You might also want to make sure your employees understand what a non-refundable ticket is. A few think it means that if the ticket isn't used, it is lost. This is typically NOT what the airlines mean. They mean you can't get the money back for the ticket. You can use the funds to purchase another ticket on the same airline within a set period of time, usually one year. You may have to pay a change fee as well. But at least the entire amount won't be lost.

Worst Practice: Doing nothing. Unused tickets are an unnecessary drain on the corporate cash flow and impact its profitability in a negative way.

The Issue: Departing Employees

From time to time, every organization will lose some of its employees. Some will leave of their own accord and others depart at the invitation of the company. The cause for the departure does not matter. The result is the same.

Sometimes people are lulled into a false sense of security if a seemingly content employee leaves for a new job. They think there is no risk. Most of the time, this is true—but not always. And of course, it is impossible to identify those instances when it is not. So, like virtually every other issue discussed in this work, there should be no exceptions when it comes to the application of best practices.

Best Practice: When an employee leaves the following should occur:

- ✓ They should turn in their last expense report before leaving
- ✓ Return any excess cash advances, if they were given any
- ✓ If you put employees in your master vendor file for expense reimbursement purposes, immediately deactivate the employee
- ✓ They should turn in their travel and entertainment credit card
- ✓ The card administrator or accounts payable should be notified of the termination immediately so they can take appropriate steps
- ✓ The bank should be notified to cancel the credit card immediately

Almost Best Practice: If you cannot manage to get this information on a timely basis from HR, periodically get a list of active cardholders from your bank. Match it up against the list of current employees and terminate any cards held by people not on the list of current employees.

Special Pointers for Accounts Payable: For this practice to work there must be coordination between HR and accounts payable. It is not enough to simply get the card back. It must be canceled at the bank. If the employee is devious, he or she will have written down the card number, expiration date and security code.

Even if he or she intends no malice, trouble can occur if they continue to carry your credit card around in their wallet. They can inadvertently use it or worse, if their wallet is stolen; your card will now be in the hands of thieves. When they report lost credit cards to the various issuers, it is almost certain they will forget about your card. Get them back. Don't leave them around where they can only cause problems.

Worst Practice: Not doing anything about travel and entertainment issues as they pertain to departing employees.

The Issue: Making Travel Reservations

Once upon a time, companies routinely required employees to book their travel arrangements through preapproved travel agencies. Larger companies negotiated special rates, based on volume usage, with airlines, hotel chains, and car rental agencies. Many big organizations continue to negotiate preferred rates.

The Internet has changed a lot of this. Employees routinely surf the Internet, finding lower airfares and hotel rates than are being offered by the corporate plan. Until recently, the prevailing wisdom was to stick with the corporate rate because, overall, the company gained more, due largely to the volume discounts offered by such plans.

Now e-commerce sites like Expedia and Travelocity have developed their own electronic equivalents of the old corporate travel office. The features they offer emulate common off-line travel services. And while these plans are not free, they are not expensive either.

Best Practice: Employees can either book on their own or through a corporate initiative, whichever the travel policy dictates. In either case, they are to:

✓ Get the best price, taking into account whether the ticket might need to be canceled

✓ Ensure policy compliance

✓ Use airlines and hotels where preferred rates have been negotiated

Almost Best Practice: None.

Special Pointers for Accounts Payable: If the company policy requires use of an agency or certain airlines or hotels, expect complaints from employees who find better rates. One way to try and limit the time spent on this issue is to include a page in the travel policy explaining the rationale for the use of the preferred carrier/hotel/car rental agency. Then when people complain, you can point them to the page for a "full explanation." This works particularly well when a very high-level executive has endorsed the policy in writing on one of the first pages.

Worst Practice: Having no policy regarding reservations.

The Issue: Reimbursing Employees

Employee reimbursement can be handled in one of several ways. These include:

✓ The employee being given a check

✓ The employee having a check mailed to their house

✓ Have the reimbursement included in their paycheck

✓ Have the reimbursement direct deposited along with payroll

✓ Have the reimbursement direct deposited to a bank account different from the one the paycheck is deposited in.

This seemingly innocuous task can create havoc in AP departments that insist on using payroll-related reimbursements. A few employees use their T&E reimbursements as "mad money," not sharing this money with their spouse. These individuals will cause quite a stir if the proposal is made to either include the reimbursements in a paycheck or have the funds direct deposited to the account where the paycheck is deposited.

Best Practice: Mandate that T&E reimbursements be direct deposited to an account, but allow employees to direct the funds to an account other than the one where payroll is deposited. By adding the flexibility feature, the number of arguments will be reduced. It is beyond the responsibility of any company to address the issue between spouses.

Almost Best Practice: None

Special Pointers for Accounts Payable: If employees insist on a check and management tolerates this, look for opportunities to get them to try the direct deposit feature, for example, when reimbursement is late and the employee needs the funds.

Worst Practice: Worst practices include:

- ✓ Reimbursing by check
- ✓ Allowing employees to pick up reimbursement checks from accounts payable

Both are an extremely inefficient use of the AP staff and causes problems when checks are misplaced or picked up by admins. Additionally, communication snafus between executives and their admins sometimes lead to a request for a second check when the first is lying on someone's desk.

The Issue: Reporting of Use of Disruptive Services

Use of ride-hailing services, such as Uber and Lyft, by business travelers is high with 74% reporting some usage by employees in an AP Now poll. Another 9% weren't sure. Yet many organizations still don't have a travel policy on the use of these services.

The major reason given for allowing use of ride-hailing services was employee convenience followed by demand by employees. Cost savings was the third reason given—but only by 21% of respondents.

The primary reason for allowing the use of car-sharing services was employee convenience followed by employee demand. Cost savings was the third reason given, but only by 20% of respondents.

One of the issues with employees using Uber, Lyft, and the myriad of other new services and apps for travel is how they account for them on their expense reports. For, if they don't report these charges correctly, it is next to impossible for the company to ferret out how much these services are being used.

Best Practice: The first step is to decide where you want these items reported. Then this information must be incorporated into the policy and shared with employees. Anecdotal evidence suggests employees are reporting these expenditures in a variety of areas including taxi, car rental and miscellaneous.

Uber reports on its website that it is registered under merchant category code 4121 for taxis and limousines. That suggests Uber and Lyft should be coded as taxis. Be aware that UberSELECT and UberBlack involve high-end sedans which translates into higher fees. If you prefer employees not use the higher-priced version, spell it out in the policy!

Each of these new services needs to be analyzed and a decision made as to whether employees should be allowed, encouraged or discouraged from using them. They should also be instructed on how to report them on their expense report. With the new short-term rentals using car2go and zip car, it is not clear whether they would be used in place of a taxi or a rental car. In some cities the rental fee is quoted in cents per minute, making it sound more like a taxi. In others, there is a daily rate.

Almost Best Practice: None.

Special Pointer for Accounts Payable: None

Worst Practice: Not establishing a policy and setting guidelines for employees.

The W-9 Headache

Chapter 17: Regulatory Issues: Information Reporting

Information reporting in the US has become a huge issue. Many believe unreported income by small businesses and independent contractors is a large cause for the budget deficit. For some time, legislators and government tax officials have looked for better ways to collect information about all income.

As some reading this might remember, the Patient Protection and Affordable Care Act of 2010 included provisions that would require Form 1099s to be filed for goods and services for everyone starting in 2012. There was much hoopla in the press and lobbying by various special interest groups. This provision was repealed at the end of 2011.

But we shouldn't celebrate too quickly. Virtually every tax professional believes this legislation will be back, probably not in the form it was presented earlier but piecemeal in the coming years. Rather than thinking we've dodged a bullet; it would be better if every organization took this as a sign to get their information reporting houses in order.

Proving that the IRS is deadly serious about getting the information it needs to collect all revenue it is owed, the service announced the addition of a new form, the 1099-NEC. This will be used to report some of the income that was formerly (prior to 2021) reported on the 1099-MISC.

We've been warned and we've got time. In this chapter we discuss:

- A Form W-9 Requirement Policy
- Collecting and Tracking Form W-9 and Form W-8 Policy
- Using IRS TIN Matching Properly

The Issue: A Form W-9/W-8 Requirement Policy

When vendors are asked to supply a Form W-9 so you can determine whether you have to report their income for tax purposes on the Form 1099, some will balk. They give all sorts of reasons as to why you shouldn't ask for this. They say things like:

- ✓ If you report my income, I'll have to pay taxes on it
- ✓ We don't give this information to anyone
- ✓ None of your competitors ask for this
- ✓ Please don't report my income

✓ It's against our company policy to provide this information

Or they just flat out refuse to provide it. Some take a more passive approach. They don't refuse but when you send them a blank W-9, they simply don't return it.

At the end of the day, if you don't get this information and report, it is your organization that will be in hot water should the IRS conduct an information audit on your tax reporting. And these audits do happen with regularity. If you are found to be out of compliance, you can be fined. And, if the IRS deems your actions were "willful disregard" of the law, the sanctions can be quite serious.

Best Practice: Require a completed, signed W-9 (or W-8 from your foreign vendors) before the first purchase order is issued. If the vendor refuses to provide it, the order should not be placed. It should also be run through IRS TIN Matching in the case of W-9s as will be discussed further in this chapter.

It should be noted that while W-9s can be provided electronically and are currently good forever or until the vendor has a change in status, W-8s are not. They are also not eligible to be run through IRS TIN Matching either.

Almost Best Practice: If you do not get the completed W-9 before the PO is issued, insist that it be obtained before the first payment is made. That is when you have the most leverage with the vendor. If you wait until after the payment is made, your influence is almost nil, especially if it turns out you will not be doing more business with the vendor in question.

Special Pointers for Accounts Payable: Some of your vendors may point out that it is not a legal requirement that they give you the completed W-9. They are correct. However, you can make it part of your terms and conditions for doing business.

If they refuse to give you the W-9 or the information verbally, you can withhold 28% and report and remit it to the IRS. Of course, since you don't have their taxpayer identification number, you won't be able to report that and the vendor in question won't get credit for the tax payment. If at all possible, avoid this step. It is messy and cumbersome, will require additional efforts and recordkeeping by your staff, and will likely antagonize the vendor in question. This will not endear you to the purchasing department either.

Worst Practice: Not collecting any taxpayer information at all.

The Issue: Collecting and Tracking Form W-9 and Form W-8 Policy

As mentioned above, asking for a W-9 from a vendor does not guarantee one will be sent. Some simply ignore the issue hoping it will go away. Others are busy and sending in the W-9 is one of those matters that falls between the cracks. Since your organization is the one to be fined if correct tax reporting is not completed, it is incumbent on the staff to make sure all the correct information is received.

Best Practice: If you follow the best practice of requiring a W-9 or W-8 before the first PO is issued or at least before the first payment is made, you are well on your way to having the information you need at 1099 time. To be effective, you must:

    ✓ Send out requests for W-9s

    ✓ Track who returned them and

    ✓ Follow up with those who have not returned them

Some are able to do this tracking in their master vendor file; others have to set up a separate mechanism to track. If you have blank fields in your master vendor file you may be able to set them to categories such as:

    ✓ W-9 sent to vendor

    ✓ Completed W-9 received from vendor

    ✓ W-9 information verified in IRS TIN Matching

By periodically checking these entries your staff will be able to do the necessary follow up to get missing information or correct data that was rejected by IRS TIN Matching.

It also should be noted that by doing this kind of tracking, you should be in a good position with the IRS should they conduct an information reporting audit on your practices and they find you are not in compliance in one facet. By showing that you are assiduously collecting W-9s, tracking their receipt and running the information through IRS TIN Matching, you will be able to demonstrate that you had good intent. This can help when trying to have fines and penalties abated. For this to help with your case you must have your tracking in place and you should document your practice in your accounts payable policy and procedures manual.

Almost Best Practice: None.

Special Pointers for Accounts Payable: If it seems to you that the accounts payable function is not getting any easier, you are correct.

Worst Practice: Worst practices include:

- ✓ Not collecting W-9s
- ✓ Sending out blank W-9s and not tracking if you ever get them back
- ✓ Not keeping your W-9s together in an easily accessible place, in case of audit
- ✓ Double checking the accuracy of your 1099s before they are issued
- ✓ When to request a new W-9
- ✓ Getting ready for the new 1099-NEC

The Issue: Using IRS TIN Matching Properly

The IRS TIN Matching is a free service offered by the IRS. It is an online interactive service offered to payers or their authorized agents. IRS TIN Matching Program does as its name suggests. It compares the TIN/Name combinations provided with information held by the IRS on its tax filing records. Organizations may use it to verify information for income subject to backup withholding and reported on Forms 1099-B, DIV, INT, MISC, OID and/or PATR.

This matching can be done online interactively for up to 25 entries at a time or in a bulk basis for up to 100,000 entries. If the latter is used the information is returned 24 hours later.

TIN Matching, under no circumstances, should be used as a phishing expedition to try and determine the correct information. If the IRS determines you are phishing, you will be kicked off the system.

The primary benefit of use of TIN Matching is a significant reduction in the number of B-Notices. Organizations that start using TIN Matching report the elimination of between 97% and 100% of all their B-Notices.

Best Practice: All information provided by vendors on a W-9 should be verified using IRS TIN Matching before the first purchase order is given. If there is a mismatch corrected information should be requested and run through TIN Matching again.

Almost Best Practice: All information provided by vendors on a W-9 should be verified using IRS TIN Matching before the first payment is made. If there is a mismatch corrected information should be requested and run through TIN Matching again.

Special Pointers for Accounts Payable: There is really no excuse for not using the IRS TIN Matching program. Anecdotal evidence suggests that the most common reason for not using TIN Matching is executive reluctance. This unwillingness stems from the fact that when registering the organization to use TIN Matching the executive is required to supply his or her social security number as well as their AGI (adjusted gross income) from their last tax return filed with the IRS.

It is not uncommon to hear executives complain, "I'm not giving them that information." In reality, they are not giving the IRS any information it does not already have. The IRS only requests this information so it can identify that the individual signing the company up for TIN Matching is who they say they are. It is for identification purposes only.

If for whatever reason, a company still does not wish to register to use IRS TIN Matching, there is another alternative. TIN Matching can be outsourced and there are a number of service providers who would be happy to take this on for your organization.

A few organizations run all their information through TIN Matching once a year right before it is time to issue 1099s. While this is better than doing nothing, it is not making the most use out of the system. Vendors are not motivated to send corrected information if you are no longer doing business with them. What's more, some smaller organizations may have gone out of business or moved leaving no forwarding address. Better to use it throughout the year correcting information as you go along.

The elimination of most, if not all B-Notices is cause enough to rush right out and register for TIN Matching.

Worst Practice: Not using IRS TIN Matching

The Issue: Double Check 1099 Accuracy before Issuing or Reporting to IRS

As you have already seen, using TIN Matching is a recommended best practice. In theory, a W-9 is good forever. So, one might think that if you run the data through TIN Matching, you should not have to repeat the task ever. However, if the vendor has a change in circumstance (say a merger, acquisition, name change etc.), that W-9 may no longer work.

Many times, companies only find out about these changes in circumstance when a B-Notice from the IRS arrives notifying them of a name TIN mismatch on the 1099 they filed.

Best Practice: Run 1099 file through IRS TIN matching before issuing 1099s every year right before you file.

Almost Best Practice: None

Special Pointer for Accounts Payable: Few vendors will think to notify their customers of a change in circumstance, if business continues as it did before the change. It is not that they are trying to hide anything, it just never occurs to them to notify customers and supply a new completed W-9 form.

Worst Practice: Neglecting to run the 1099 file through TIN Matching before filing.

The Issue: When to Request a New Form W-9

A Form W-9 is a form created by the IRS for use by organizations who need to collect tax payer information for reporting to the IRS. Once the information has been collected it is good forever – unless the provider of that information has what is referred to as a "change in circumstance." This might be a merger, acquisition, change in legal structure etc.

Best Practice: Collect taxpayer identification information on a W-9 form, using the most current form, once. Since it is unlikely your vendors will notify you when there is a change in circumstance, request a new W-9 anytime the vendor notifies you of other changes, such as a change in address or a change of bank account.

Why? Because often these changes accompany a change in legal circumstance that will invalidate the taxpayer information you currently have on file. By getting the new Form W-9, you will be able to ascertain whether or not there has been a change. If you can't tell, run it through IRS TIN Matching for the final determination.

Almost Best Practice: None

Special Pointer for Accounts Payable: Alas, very few vendors think to tell their customers about these changes. The customers learn the hard way, when a penalty notice shows up. Avoid having to deal with penalty notices and B-Notices from the IRS by taking this one simple step.

Worst Practice: Not requesting a new W-9 when there are indications that there has been a change in circumstance.

The Issue: The New Form 1099-NEC

If you are a company located in the United States, and you are reading this prior to 2021, you know that there is a new 1099-NEC form from the IRS. This will replace some of the reporting that was done on the form 1099-MISC. to adequately report in January 2021, data will have to be tracked in a different manner than it was tracked prior when all the information was reported on the MISC form. This will require massive system changes for most organizations.

Best Practice: Begin preparation for the new form as soon as possible. This means if you are reading this right after the book was published in August or September 2020, and you have not started preparation, immediately contact someone in it to get started.

Almost Best Practice: None.

Special Pointer for Accounts Payable: if you have done any independent contractor income reporting to the IRS in the past you know that every year, it seems, the IRS changes the rules somewhat. Some years the changes are minor, others a little bit more complicated. This year the change is massive. So, the sooner you begin working on it the better. For most, this will require IT changes, so do no wait.

This issue will be complicated if once again, accounts payable teams are forced to work remotely due to coronavirus or other issues.

Worst Practice: Waiting until January 2021 to address the matter.

Male AP Super Hero

Chapter 18: Regulatory Issues: Unclaimed Property

Unclaimed property, also referred to as abandoned property or escheat, is a requirement that any property that is abandoned or unclaimed be turned over to the state. The rules regarding which state gets the property, when it has to be turned over, and a myriad of other details vary from state to state. When it comes to the accounts payable function, un-cashed checks are considered abandoned property.

The rationale behind turning unclaimed property over to the states is that they will hold it until the rightful owner steps forward to claim it. That's why the states are putting information about the abandoned property they hold on the Internet. It helps people track down money that is owed to them. However, not all the information is online and much of the older data remains in paper or microfiche records.

States everywhere are looking for every last nickel they can get their hands on so unclaimed property audits are viewed as a source of revenue, despite what you may see in the newspapers.

Since unclaimed property gets remitted to the state of the last known address of the owner and if that is not known the state of incorporation, unclaimed property is very important to the state of Delaware, where it makes up over 10% of the annual state budget. And Delaware is not alone.

In this chapter we look at best practices related to the:

- Reporting and Remitting Unclaimed Property
- Performing Due Diligence for Unclaimed Property
- Using Social Media to Track Rightful Owners of Unclaimed Property

The Issue: Reporting and Remitting Unclaimed Property

Experts estimate that only about one-third of all organizations who should be reporting and remitting unclaimed property actually do so. This massive under-reporting provides the already-cash-strapped states with a golden opportunity. Many rely on third-party audit firms who work on a contingency basis. These firms perform unclaimed property audits for the states, keeping a percentage of what they recover.

These audits can go back to the date of the last closed audit. If you've never had one that means they can go back to the day your company opened its doors. But most states are not that cruel. They limit their look back period to 20 or 30 years. Now, if you are thinking that you don't have records going back that far, you are in for another rude surprise.

If you don't have records for them to audit, the states will gladly estimate what you owe. This is not apt to turn out well for you so you'll have to hire your own statistician to do an estimate and then negotiate a settlement. You'll not only have to pay what is owed, you'll also owe interest. This can turn out to be a serious amount of money.

Now those reading this may be scratching their head wondering how the state will be able to return the unclaimed property over to its rightful owner if an estimate is made on what is owed. How would either party know who the rightful owner was? That is a cogent point. Money turned over as the result of an estimation process cannot be associated with an owner. Hence, it can never be recovered and will remain forever in the state's coffers.

Best Practice: Report and remit your unclaimed property to the appropriate state at the appropriate time. Conduct your due diligence as described later in this chapter. I

Almost Best Practice: However, if you are not currently reporting, don't just start reporting. Get an expert to help you. The states will pick up on the fact that it is your first-time reporting and an auditor will show up to look through our back records.

Special Pointers for Accounts Payable: The states have claimed that they will audit every organization that falls within their reporting environ. Not reporting and remitting is only putting off the inevitable.

However, if you are not currently reporting, don't just start reporting. Get an expert to help you. Many of the states have voluntary disclosure initiatives and the expert will negotiate on your behalf, trying to get the penalties and interest reduced. Periodically, some of the states will run amnesty programs. Again, get an expert to help you. These unchartered waters are choppy and the money you pay the expert to get you in compliance will be well worth it.

There is an ugly practice that occurs in the unclaimed property arena. A third-party auditor will contact your firm offering to get your company in compliance at no cost. Don't be fooled by this offer. The auditor is in all likelihood working for the state and will be paid a percentage of what is recovered during your audit.

They will not operate in your best interest nor will they do the necessary research to disqualify items that are really not unclaimed property. Unfortunately, they will probably be back this time wearing their official state hat. So, be prepared to hire your own expert.

There are two additional, somewhat distressing trends emerging in the compliance arena. The first is that some of the third-party auditors work for multiple states. They may perform audits for all at the same time or come back a second or third time.

The second issue relates to the states need for money. Some of their own auditors now handle multiple issues. So, for example, the state may send in an auditor to do an information reporting audit and he or she may poke around to also determine if an income tax or unclaimed property audit might bring in additional revenue.

Get all your ducks in a row. Do what you are supposed to do and this will not be a problem.

Worst Practice: Worst practices include:

- ✓ Claiming your own abandoned property when you are not reporting
- ✓ Writing off un-cashed checks to miscellaneous income
- ✓ Not reporting and remitting your organization's unclaimed property

The Issue: Performing Due Diligence for Unclaimed Property

The states really don't want you turning over funds to them that will immediately be claimed by its rightful owner. They expect the holder of the funds to do some due diligence to try and find the rightful owner, before turning funds over.

Best Practice: The sooner you follow up on un-cashed checks, the easier your work is likely to be. Many organizations follow up at the six-month mark, but 90 days is probably a better option. Send a registered letter with a self-addressed stamped envelope inquiring about the payment.

Save all the documentation. This includes the notification of the registered letter, any returned mail, and the response from the payee. This is important if you decide a payment is a duplicate and reverse it. It is also important if you write the amount off to miscellaneous income. If you can't provide the documentation, the auditor is likely to decide it should be turned over as abandoned property.

Almost Best Practice: If you don't follow up at 90 days, do so at the six-month mark, as described above.

Special Pointers for Accounts Payable: Note that one way to eliminate un-cashed checks is to minimize, if not eliminate, checks written. The best way to do this is to move your payments to an electronic platform paying through the ACH. If you do have a bad or inactive bank account number, you find that out the next day and can take action.

If you can move the bulk of your payments away from paper, you'll greatly reduce your unclaimed property exposure and due diligence required efforts. This is an added bonus few take into consideration when evaluating a move to electronic payments.

Also note that most states have a different dormancy period for payroll checks than they do for accounts payable items. Thus, you'll have to send the money in for the payroll checks earlier than the accounts payable items.

Also be aware, that some of the states have been changing their dormancy periods, virtually always shortening them. Dormancy periods are the amount of time you must hold the funds before turning them over to the states.

This trend is expected to continue. This means you need to regularly check the states websites or other resources to find out if the dormancy periods have changed.

Worst Practice: Worst practices include:

- ✓ Sending abandoned property to the state too early or too late
- ✓ Not performing the due diligence required

Some have tried sending the funds early, not wanting to keep track of them for the entire due diligence period, which for accounts payable checks can be several years. The states return the money. They don't want it early and they don't want it late. They simply want it when it is due.

The Issue: Using Social Media to Track Rightful Owners of Unclaimed Property

As you've probably figure out by now, the due diligence efforts described above can be quite paper and manual intensive and the price for completing them can add up. In this time of electronic communication spanning continents, surely there has to be some way to harness this technology to reduce manual efforts with regards to unclaimed property.

Best Practice: Use social media sites to try and find rightful owners. This is especially effective when it comes to un-cashed payroll checks, which are typically the last check when an employee leaves the organization. Often, they don't realize they are owed that money and move without making arrangements.

A number of companies have had great success locating former employees using LinkedIn and Facebook. Once the potential owner of the un-cashed check is identified, they are approached online with an inquiry if they were the same person who used to work for the company in question. On LinkedIn this is even easier as most participants list their former employers.

Almost Best Practice: None – yet!

Special Pointers for Accounts Payable: Obviously, some care has to be exercised when approaching folks on social media sites. If you ask "are you the John Jones who used to work for ABC company? We've got some money for you" you are going to get a positive response regardless of whether you've got the right person or not.

Also, some companies block social media sites because they don't want employees wasting countless hours socializing when they should be working. If this is the case in your organization you can either ask that the block be lifted on a particular account or perhaps the research could be done when working remotely.

By using this method for identifying owners of your abandoned property, you save the expense associated with the more manual approach to due diligence. Combine this approach with a move to electronic payments and you'll see the amount of property your organization has to turn over to the state dwindle, hopefully to almost nothing.

Worst Practice: Not exercising proper caution when approaching potential former employees.

Female AP Super Hero

Chapter 19: Regulatory Issues: Other

Female AP Super Hero The number of regulatory issues that need to be considered when addressing the accounts payable function continues to grow. Typically, we only think of the tax reporting, i.e. 1099 issues when it comes to regulatory matters in accounts payable. But there are more. In this issue we take a look at the following:

- Proper Handling of Sales and Use Tax
- Regular OFAC Checking
- Foreign Corrupt Practices Act (FCPA) Monitoring

The Issue: Proper Handling of Sales and Use Tax

Sales tax is a tax on the retail sale of tangible personal property. Keep in mind that sale tax is only paid on retail sales. It is also charged on certain services. Which services are taxed varies from one taxing locale to the next.

Cynics claim that use tax was created for those situations where the states believe they have the right to charge sales tax but legally can't. Hence, if you normally would have paid sales tax, but the vendor didn't charge it because it does not have nexus in the locale in question, you are required to accrue use tax and pay it at the appropriate time.

Use tax is charged by many (but not all) states on the "privilege of storing." In this case, storage means the purchaser's holding or controlling property brought in from out of state that is not intended for resale. The rules for what is and is not subject to use tax are very complicated and vary from state to state. It is imperative that the AP professionals responsible for sales and use tax learn what their state rules are.

In recent years, with the advent of online retailing, the issue of sales tax has become a hot topic. The states want the revenue from sales tax on online purchases but the online retailers claim they have no nexus and thus do not have to collect and remit sales tax. The concept of click-thru nexus has been introduced and it appears that ever so slowly the online retailers are losing this battle.

More than a few companies have no formal policies and procedures for the sales and use tax responsibility. An auditor who finds a company in noncompliance is likely to be more sympathetic to a company that has a policy in place than one who has ignored the issue. The existence of a policy indicates that the company intends to pay its sales and use taxes, even if it does not always do it correctly. The lack of a formal policy implies that the company has no plan to pay. Thus, the existence of a policy is a company's first defense against an aggressive tax collector.

There is one last very good reason to have a policy in place. A growing number of states now conduct multi-faceted audits. The auditor that comes in to review your organization's income taxes may also glance at your sales tax procedures and perhaps your unclaimed property reporting. If you are found wanting in any of those secondary areas, he or she will either conduct a full-blown audit of those practices or alert their colleagues in the applicable area. The bottom line is that it is getting more and more difficult to skirt regulatory requirements—so don't try.

Best Practice: Incorporate a strong policy of verifying sales tax on invoices and accruing use tax where sales tax was not charged but should have. Regularly, verify rates and other changes.

Almost Best Practice: None; there is no half-way measure. Proper handling of both sales and use tax are something every organization must do.

Special Pointers for Accounts Payable: Realize that sales taxes continually change. With over 7,000 taxing entities in the US, it's a massive job keeping on top of the changes in rates and the changes in items taxed. And, unfortunately, there is no uniformity in what's taxed from one jurisdiction to the next.

If an invoice doesn't have sales tax included, resist the temptation to add sales tax to an invoice before paying it. Typically, organizations that follow this practice want to follow with the law but don't want the hassle of accruing, reporting and remitting use tax. There are several reasons why this is a bad practice. For starters, you might be wrong in your assessment that sales tax is due. Then you've paid money you really didn't owe.

More often than not, you are correct in your assessment. However, the vendor did not add sales tax to the invoice because they do not have an obligation to report the sales tax in your state as they probably don't have nexus. Most importantly, they will not report or remit the tax. When you are audited by a state sales tax auditor, you will be found deficient, have to pay the tax and any penalties they may choose to accrue. The fact that you paid it to the vendor will be your problem. You will be left to try and recoup it on your own. Paying it to the vendor is just as bad as paying it to the wrong state. The right state will demand its money and you will be left on your own to try and recoup it from the state you paid the funds to incorrectly.

Worst Practice: Worst practices include:

- ✓ Ignoring the sales and use tax issues
- ✓ Paying all sales tax to one state, instead of paying it to the states where it is owed
- ✓ Adding sales tax to a payment for an item you will owe use tax on, counting on the supplier to understand what you did and pay the sales tax appropriately
- ✓ Not checking employees' expense reports for items that might

be subject to sales and use tax withholding

✓ Not checking purchases made on p-cards to ensure that the appropriate sales and/or use tax was withheld

The Issue: Regular OFAC Checking

The OFAC regulations pertain to the making of payments to terrorists and other blocked parties. When this issue is mentioned, more than a few think it doesn't pertain to them because, "of course they wouldn't do business with a terrorist." However, it is not that simple. Terrorists masquerade as normal companies, with innocent sounding names.

The Office of Foreign Assets Control (OFAC) of the US Department of the Treasury administers and enforces economic and trade sanctions based on US foreign policy and national security goals against targeted foreign countries and regimes, terrorists, international narcotics traffickers, those engaged in activities related to the proliferation of weapons of mass destruction, and other threats to the national security, foreign policy or economy of the United States.

The Department of the Treasury produces a list of entities which US organizations are not permitted to do business with. This list is regularly updated, sometimes as frequently as several times a day.

Best Practice: Before each payment is made, check the OFAC list to make sure none of your vendors have been added to the OFAC list. Sometimes when this is mentioned, people are a bit taken back. But, you are tasked with not paying terrorists. And, since that list is updated very frequently, the only way to make sure you don't make such a payment is to check the list every single time you make a payment.

The list can be downloaded from the Department of Treasury's website. A process can be automated whereby the list is updated right before your check run. Then all payments should be verified against the list. It's not as hard as it might sound at first glance.

Almost Best Practice: Some organizations run their entire master vendor file against the OFAC list once a month. While this might allow a few payments to slip through, it is a huge step in the right direction.

Other organizations check all new vendors against the OFAC list and then never check again. While this is better than doing nothing, it is not really sufficient to be in compliance with the law.

Special Pointers for Accounts Payable: Expect to get many false positives when running your vendors against the list. When you get what looks to be a match, you'll need to do a little investigating. Here's an example. When checking the list for a talk I was giving, I discovered a company on the list called The Bamboo Company. Now, there are many companies with this name in a number of different countries and most are perfectly honest. That's why you will need to do a little more investigating once you find a potential match.

This is another example of how terrorists use names for their organization that make them sound legitimate. It is also why this type of checking on a regular basis is imperative.

Worst Practice: Completely ignoring this issue.

The Issue: Foreign Corrupt Practices Act (FCPA) Monitoring

A similar, but very different, issue is that of the anti-bribery legislation. While this legislation has been on the books since the late seventies, it has become a hot issue in recent years. The press has had a field day covering several large cases where well-known companies were found to have violated the FCPA strictures.

The FCPA was originally passed in 1977, and later amended in 1988 and 1998. Specifically, its anti-bribery provisions prohibit the offer or promise to pay bribes to foreign officials, foreign political parties or party officials as well as candidates for political office. Also covered is the payment or authorization of payment to these parties. The payments are prohibited when the intent is to obtain or retain business or to direct business to a particular person.

Also prohibited are indirect payments.

The legislation has one exception. Payments made to facilitate or expedite the performance of "routine governmental action" are permitted. Typically this covers obtaining permits, licenses or other official documents qualifying a person to do business in a foreign country, processing government documents such as visas and work orders, providing policy protection, mail pickup and delivery or scheduling inspections associated with contract performance or transit of goods, providing phone service, power and water supply, loading and unloading cargo or protecting perishable products or commodities from deterioration, etc.

When most people think of bribery they think of the exchange of money for as the medium of exchange. But this does not have to be, especially when talking about the Foreign Corrupt Practices Act (FCPA), In fact, the Act defines a bribe very broadly as "anything of value." So, in addition to money, this might include:

- ✓ An offer of employment for the recipient or someone designated by the recipient
- ✓ Discounts
- ✓ Gifts
- ✓ Lavish meals and other entertainment (including trips)
- ✓ Stock
- ✓ A commission
- ✓ Property

What's more, the bribe is still a bribe if it is paid through a third party or is a future payment. These considerations make it all the more difficult for accounts payable to ferret out payments that are really bribes. It is also why it is important to scrutinize expense reimbursements closely.

Best Practice: The first step is to train the accounts payable staff to look at invoices, expense reports and any other vehicle related to the making of payments for anything that looks like it might be a bribe. The legislation is very complicated so it is important that everyone who works with these payments understands what they are looking for.

Some of these payments will appear on an expense report so may slide under the radar unless the staff knows to look for them. Once the staff has identified potential items, they should be brought to the attention of management for further investigation and follow-up, if it is determined that something is amiss. Under no circumstances should the invoice processor discuss a potential questionable item with the person who received the payment, submitted the payment or approved the payment.

Almost Best Practice: None. This is another one of those issues that has to be done in full to be in compliance with the law.

Special Pointers for Accounts Payable: Be aware that many of the items will turn out to be false positives. That's why it is imperative that further investigation be done and if there is an item that was paid inappropriately, management be involved. This is an extremely delicate matter that if handled incorrectly could result in a lot of trouble for the organization with the Department of Justice. No one wants to go down that road.

Worst Practice: Ignoring the issue completely.

AP's Love Affair with Two Screens

Chapter 20: Technology

Gone are the days when accounts payable's technology plan consisted of getting the hand-me-down personal computers when other departments upgraded to newer models. Today, even those organizations not on the leading-edge recognize the need to equip their accounts payable staff with modern equipment capable of working with intricate programs and secure high-speed Internet access.

In this chapter, we take a look at the following issues:

- An Accounts Payable Technology Plan
- Handling of Emailed Invoices
- Invoice Automation

- Use of Mobile Devices in Accounts Payable

The Issue: An Accounts Payable Technology Plan

Unfortunately, many organizations still have a haphazard approach to technology issues in accounts payable. They have no formal game plan, simply lurching forward with makeshift training as needed. Rather than sitting back and planning to make sure the entire staff has the equipment they need and the training required, they only step in at the last minute, leaving many of their processes limping along less efficient than they could be.

To be fair, the budget allocations necessary to purchase hardware, software and training are sometimes beyond the control of the accounts payable manager. But this does not mean that he or she cannot make recommendations based on solid explanations and ultimately influence the inclusion of some funds for the needed technology.

What's more, with the development of the Internet, there are some features that do not require funding. Additionally, there are training and other resources that either cost very little or nothing.

Best Practice: Develop a strategic plan that addresses the hardware requirements of the staff. Of course, this cannot be done until a thorough evaluation has been made of software requirements. This includes not only identifying the software in question, but also the cost of upgrades and training, if any. While the accounts payable manager can make recommendations, they typically do not have the final say on this issue.

As part of this strategic plan, identify the software that the staff should be able to use and consider whether any training is needed. Too often, expensive software is purchased and then because no training is offered, only a small percentage of its capabilities are ever utilized. In fact sometimes, because of lack of training, employees are not even aware the software sitting on their computers could perform certain tasks that would make them more efficient and effective.

What follows is a short list of software everyone working in accounts payable should be able to use. You probably have additional entries to the list.

- ✓ Accounting software used by the organization
- ✓ Word
- ✓ Excel
- ✓ Database management, such as Access
- ✓ PowerPoint (or other presentation software)

In addition, they should know how to:

- ✓ Write macros
- ✓ Create pivot tables
- ✓ Attend online meetings using Zoom, Teams, GoToMeeting, and whatever other new product hits the market.
- ✓ Post job listings on LinkedIn
- ✓ Search for owners of Unclaimed Property on LinkedIn (and possibly Facebook)

Google has developed its own version of the Microsoft Office programs (Docs, Sheets etc.) and learning these is a nice touch. Since they seem to be very similar to Office, it is not overly difficult.

Don't assume your staff knows these products intimately. Most people, unless they've had some training or are especially adventurous when it comes to technology, only know the basics.

Finally, be aware, that technology is anything but a static issue. To put the matter in perspective, consider that Google began as a research project in 1996. The company incorporated in 1998 and only started selling adwords in 2000. Twitter came into being in 2006, YouTube in 2005 and Skype was first released in 2003.

Technology is making huge inroads in our lives and the accounts payable function is part of that revolution. Therefore, it is critical that everyone be alert to the next big innovation and be ready to learn how to use it and how to integrate it into the work process to make accounts payable more efficient than ever.

Many companies are starting to look at the technology employees have at home and make an investment in it or in upgrading it. This is due to the problems they encountered when the staff worked remotely during the COVID crisis. Technology considerations should be part of any remote working policy an organization creates.

Almost Best Practice: Providing training for all these different products can be tricky especially if you are dealing with a limited budget. But that does not have to be a deal breaker. There are free and low-cost webinars, if you look.

Also, don't overlook YouTube, especially if you have a question about a small feature of Excel or one of the other Office products. There are many short videos posted on YouTube explaining how to use various functions. This is also true of accounting issues, accounts payable issues and other technology questions.

Pointers for Accounts Payable: Many organizations block websites such as Facebook, YouTube and sometimes even LinkedIn. They do this as a matter of corporate policy, sometimes because employees have spent too much time on these sites involved in non-company activities. If your organization is one of those, you can either:

- ✓ Talk to management to see if you can have the restrictions lifted at least on one computer explaining why you need access
- ✓ Access the sites from home and handle the needed tasks there

Worst Practice: Ignoring the technology issue or trying to stick your head in the sand and pretending the rest of the world isn't changing.

The Issue: Handling of Emailed Invoices

Electronic invoicing, or e-invoicing, means different things to different people. Some folks use the term to refer to automated invoice processing systems, usually run by third parties. But, most take a more inclusive approach and use the term to include invoices e-mailed by the vendor to the customer, usually in the form of a PDF file.

Research by Accounts Payable Now and Tomorrow reveals that the vast majority of companies now receive at least a few invoices by e-mail. This growing practice puts some form of e-invoicing within the reach of virtually every organization.

Best Practice: Develop a policy for encouraging vendors who are not using third party e-invoicing systems to e-mail their invoices. This benefits not only the supplier but the customer as well. Invoices are received quickly and can be routed for approvals. If the company is using an imaging process, it saves them from the time and expense of having to do the imaging themselves.

Establish a routine for handling invoices emailed by suppliers. It might include the following:

- ✓ Set up one e-mail address to receive invoices from suppliers
- ✓ Provide this email address to suppliers, either in the Welcome Packet or annual letter to vendors.
- ✓ Vendors should be informed that only invoices should be sent to this address. Nothing else sent there will be forwarded.
- ✓ Vendors should be instructed not to send a second invoice by snail mail. Be aware that some will disregard this directive.
- ✓ The e-mail address should not be an address associated with an individual but rather one that can be access by several people
- ✓ Different people can be assigned to forward the e-mails in the account on different days and can fill in for each other when someone is out or on vacations
- ✓ Upon receipt of the invoice, it should immediately be reviewed and forwarded to the appropriate party for approval.

If you have a fax number set up to receive invoices, and you should, connect it to an e-fax facility. This will take the paper invoice, convert it to an e-mail and you'll never see a piece of paper.

Almost Best Practice: For those who still prefer the paper, and there are more than a few such companies, establish a routine similar to the one described above for handling e-mailed invoices. The reason for this is that some vendors are now refusing to mail invoices claiming it is too expensive.

Thus, whether an organization wants to or not, they are going to be forced to deal with e-mailed invoices. So, it is best to have a policy. And, those who establish a policy for vendors insistent on emailing invoices may find that they prefer this method of delivery. When that happens they will then begin to encourage all vendors to deliver invoices electronically.

Special Pointers for Accounts Payable: With the advent of the PDF invoice, as well as advances made by technology, it is now very easy to have many original looking invoices. What's more, fewer and fewer suppliers are marking the second invoices they send as Duplicate or Copy. Hence, we need to change the way we look for duplicate invoices.

What's more, with a sizeable number of suppliers both snail mail and e-mailing the same invoice, duplicate checking routines have never been more important. Stringent coding standards and standardized routines for processing invoices are important. For it is no longer possible to identify a duplicate or copied invoice simply by looking at it.

Worst Practice: Worst practices include:

- ✓ Refusing to accept e-mailed invoices
- ✓ Not establishing an e-mail address for invoices to be sent
- ✓ Allowing the use of employees' email accounts to receive invoices (and when they leave the company those invoices end up nowhere

The Issue: Invoice Automation

Invoice automation has come a long way in just a few short years. Typically, the process includes an imaging and workflow, although even the imaging portion has decreased as much of the information is delivered electronically. Although some large companies have developed their own proprietary models, most of the invoice automation today is handled by third party specialists. The price for this service has dropped drastically and many now offer their services on a pay-as-you-go basis.

What's more implementation time has also dropped along with time needed by in-house IT staff. While their involvement is usually required, the amount of time they must devote to getting these invoice automation projects up and running is minimal. Some of these systems can be up and running six to eight weeks after a contract is signed.

Best Practice: Learn as much as you can about the different vendor models available. Wherever possible attend vendor demos so you can get a good feeling for what is available and what service would work best with your organization's invoices. Then take a look at the pricing. You may be surprised to discover that not only does the service provider want your company's business, but the cost savings associated with using the service is larger than you think. Organizations that have a good portion of their invoices handled through an automated process are able to free up staffers to work on more value-add projects.

Almost Best Practice: None.

Special Pointers for Accounts Payable: Many of the third-party invoice automation systems handle e-mailed invoices without any difficulty. Others will handle the paper invoices you still receive, without a hitch.

Worst Practice: Ignoring this issue.

The Issue: Use of Mobile Devices in Accounts Payable

Technology has made huge inroads in the consumer market as well as the B2B world. Sometimes the lines between the two blurs. This has happened with the advent of Smartphones and tablets. Many of these devices are being purchased by individuals rather than businesses.

What's more, more than a few of the individuals who buy these devices, end up using them for work. While that might not seem like a problem, especially for the company who didn't have to pay for them, it could be when the security issues are considered.

Consider the following data from an Accounts Payable Now & Tomorrow survey. Of those surveyed,

- ✓ 74% owned smartphones
- ✓ 79% paid for those phones themselves
- ✓ 58% of those who paid for it themselves, check work e-mail on them

When it comes to tablets, the statistics are even more alarming.

- ✓ 50% own tablets
- ✓ 92% paid for tablets themselves
- ✓ 75% of those who paid for tablets themselves, check work e-mail on them

While it is a good sign that so many people involved in the accounts payable function are so interested in technology and willing to pay for it out of their own pockets, we can't overlook the security issues, especially given the rise in ACH fraud, most notably corporate account takeovers.

Anecdotal evidence from practitioners reveals that some managers are releasing ACH and wires from their Smartphones and tablets during meetings. Again, while the efficiency of multi-tasking is great, the security concerns should not be ignored.

Best Practice: Create a corporate policy regarding the use of personal devices (Smartphones and tablets) for company business. If the practice is permitted, then the devices must have anti-fraud and anti-virus software installed and updated on a regular basis. If these devices are to be allowed for company transactions, they should be included in whatever regime is used for all company computers when it comes to security measures.

If the organization does not wish to include these devices in its security measures, a policy should be established prohibiting the use of personal devices for company business.

Almost Best Practice: None.

Special Pointers for Accounts Payable: This is just one example of the rapidly changing technology world and how it affects the accounts payable function. In all likelihood, employees believe they are being helpful when using personal devices for company business. However, they have not thought the issue through.

As time goes on, there will be an increasing number of issues just like this. And, every organization needs to continually evaluate these issues, see if and how they affect their organization and develop policies to address the new concerns.

Worst Practice: Ignoring this issue.

The Issue: Upgrade Employees Technology at Home

Before 2020, few gave any thought to the technology accounts payable employees had at home. Only a small group worked remotely, and those folks mostly did it only one or two days a week. What's more, it was viewed by many as a privilege. So few even mentioned that perhaps they'd like or need help with technology for fear of losing that perk.

Then COVID hit and many had to take their work home with very little notice. I would not have liked to be the folks working on corporate IT help desks during that time. Here are just a few of the technology-related problems, AP Now readers reported during that period:

- IT helping remotely
- It took almost a week for my system to work successfully and still there are many glitches.
- Technology at home is not as good as technology at work
- Don't have two screens at home
- Bringing desktops home – office networked, home wireless access
- Buying equipment, that was not necessarily up to company

standards for laptops or printers

- Spouses/children sharing a computer

- Security standards (or lack thereof at home)

- Employee could only view a portion of an invoice and have to keep enlarging it on the screen in order to work it.

- The connectivity is terrible.

- Company firewalls keep kicking us out and they do not allow us to print at home.

The lack of appropriate equipment meant some people worked longer hours just to get the same amount of work done. There was also the issue of cyber security. It will be some time before we know the full extent of any damage related to that issue.

Best Practice: Since many will be working remotely, at least part of the time, companies need to invest in the technology their employees will use under these circumstances. For the most part, this will not be a huge investment. Whether the staff will follow the best practice of working home remotely one or more days a week or not, this will still be an issue.

For at some point in the future, there will be another crisis, forcing everyone to work from home and we all need to be ready. That crisis could be weather-related or health-related or something else. While no one knows when it will hit, it is certain that at some point in the future, we will once again be working remotely, whether we like it or not. And the next time, it might be more severe and there may be no leeway to designate the accounts payable staff as essential and therefore able to go into the office.

Almost Best Practice: Look for simple workarounds. Sometimes, employees will have an old computer at home, that might have a monitor for example. With a little ingenuity, and perhaps an extra cable or two, your tech people might be able to help your staffers hook up that old second screen. This won't always work, but it is certainly worth trying.

Special Pointer for Accounts Payable: Prior to the COVID crisis, no one really gave this any thought. But, after living through it, the issues that emerged proved that a small investment might be a good idea. For a few dollars, you can make your employees comfortable and improve productivity. It was eye opening to see how many accounting people complained about missing their two screens on their work computer.

Worst Practice: Ignoring the issue

Missing Co-Workers when Working Remotely

Chapter 21: Communications/Vendor Relations

The accounts payable function is an integral part of the finance and accounting chain. To operate efficiently, it also has to communicate regularly with vendors. In this chapter, we investigate best practices related to:

- Communicating Relevant Information to Vendors
- Communicating with Internal Customers
- Working with Purchasing
- Customer Service in Accounts Payable

The Issue: Communicating Relevant Information to Vendors

While payment and invoice status information is important to vendors, it is not the only information needed by vendors. If the vendors are not educated in the beginning about what they need to do to get paid, the payment process is likely to be rocky – especially from the vendors' point of view. Similarly, when a payment is sent, if it is not for the exact amount of the invoice, the vendor is likely to have questions. And, those questions will result in numerous phone calls to accounts payable. This leads to poor vendor relations and inefficiencies in the accounts payable department. Hence, anything that can be done to improve the information flow to vendors not only improves vendor relations, but also the efficiency of the department.

Best Practice: From the day the relationship starts, vendors need to have all the information they need about your processes, procedures and requirements. This can be done utilizing one or more of the following vehicles:

✓ A welcome letter spelling out your requirements, such as

- Where invoice should be sent
- Special terms
- Bill-to address
- Other special requirements

✓ A handbook that details requirements for payment. This can be quite detailed, as is the case with some of the bigger retailers.

✓ A spot on the website that spells out the information that is included in the manual or in the welcome letter. This allows the vendor to know what it is getting into before the fact.

The other piece of information that vendors require is a list of:

✓ Who the accounts payable contacts are

✓ What these individuals' phone numbers are

✓ What their e-mail addresses are

Depending on how you handle vendor inquiries, this can be the same person who processes their invoices or someone who does nothing but address vendor questions.

While this may seem obvious, it is one of the issues that vendors repeatedly bring up when asked about when discussing relations with their customers. Needless to say, this information should be updated and shared with vendors whenever there is a change.

Letting the vendor know what is expected, is only the first step.

As discussed previously, providing a self-service function that allows vendors to check on payment and invoice status is another best practice, especially if dispute resolution can be incorporated into that process.

The other area that can be improved relatively easily is the sharing of information with vendors when anything other than the full amount is paid on an invoice. Now make no mistake about it, sharing the information will not end the phone calls, but it will reduce the number of phone calls needed to resolve issues. Most deductions taken by companies will fall into several broad categories. While some of the deductions, including:

✓ Early payment discounts

✓ Damaged goods

✓ Short shipments

✓ Penalties

might be common place, others will be unique to the company or industry. Prepare a simple form that can be included with the payment. If at all possible, have this information printed on the remittance advice part of the check. If you are paying electronically, send this information along in an e-mail to the person handling cash application at your vendor.

When the vendor receives the data, it may still call. But, the call asking the reason for the deduction and the ensuing research will be eliminated.

Almost Best Practice: If the company cannot share information about short payments easily, the accounts payable staff should make some simple notes detailing the reasons for the deductions. Then, when the inevitable phone calls do come, the staff can refer to the notes and easily respond to the inquiry. Given the nature of technology today, this data should be kept in a shared database, so everyone has access to it and can respond to calls on a timely basis.

Special Pointers for Accounts Payable: Calls about payments from vendors will continue regardless of what best practices are instituted by accounts payable. However, the number of these phone calls can be reduced greatly by some of these customer service initiatives. If, for example, the payment status information is available on the Internet, take the time to walk the vendor through checking it, when they call. Yes, it is quicker to check it yourself. However, the time spent walking the vendor through the process is a good investment, as this vendor will not need to call again.

Worst Practices: Some companies don't share information about deductions with vendors, hoping that the amounts will be so small that the vendor won't call. Sometimes they are correct. But more often than not, the vendor will call and call numerous times until the issue is resolved. This also leads to frayed vendor relations and could ultimately result in higher prices or a key supplier deciding not to bid when the next RFP goes out.

The Issue: Communicating with Internal Customers

Companies where the accounts payable department has a poor image as well as poor relations with other departments can attribute part of the problem back to the fact that the rest of the company doesn't really know what accounts payable needs in order to get payments made, as well as key cutoff dates. This is an issue that is easily remedied.

Best Practice: Accounts payable needs to communicate its requirements to others in the company. This can be done by:

- ✓ Sharing the AP policy and procedures manual
- ✓ Periodically sending around a short informative AP newsletter
- ✓ Publishing the names and contact information of the staffers in accounts payable
- ✓ Publishing the cutoff dates for T&E payments and vendor payments

The accounts payable department should have a few pages on the company's Intranet site. The information indicated above should be included on it for all to see. Transparency should be the name of the game. If the AP policy and procedures manual is long, and many are, a shorter synopsis can be included on the web site and/or in a memo to the rest of the company. It is unrealistic to expect others to wade through it to find the information they need.

Larger companies might want to assign one or more people to a customer service function and answer questions the rest of the company might have with accounts payable related issues.

As discussed in other parts of this book, the policy and procedures manual should be updated periodically. Perhaps input from other affected areas could be sought the next time the update is done. Those having input are more likely to conform to the policy than those who don't.

The old adage of walking a mile in someone else's shoes is a good one for accounts payable and other departments. Occasionally purchasing and accounts payable are at odds. By having representatives from each department work for a day or two in the other department can lead to a greater understanding of the other's problems. This is also a good idea since the two groups need to work closely.

Accounts payable should track errors to find the root cause of problems. With this data, they can identify weak points as well as other departments that may be causing problems. This does not have to be a negative. Let's say that with the error information, it becomes apparent that one purchasing agent is responsible for numerous voided checks. By meeting that agent and reviewing the process, not only can the situation be rectified, the relationship may be also strengthened.

Whenever a new system is rolled out, representatives from accounts payable should be sent to interact with other departments to ensure that everyone knows how to use it properly.

Almost Best Practice: Send the staff to customer service courses to help them deal with difficult situations, making sure they understand that they are not the customer.

Special Pointers for Accounts Payable: The very nature of the tasks handled in accounts payable make it likely that there will be conflicts from time to time. These can be both with other departments as well as vendors. The goal should be to handle these sticky situations with finesse and tact. Vendors will sometimes try and get accounts payable to pay them earlier than their contracts stipulate, other employees will occasionally blame accounts payable for late payments they caused, and employees who are tardy about their T&E reports will then try and hurry the process when their credit card bills show up.

By recognizing that these situations will arise and dealing with each separately, relations with internal customers will improve. But don't expect an overnight improvement. It will take time.

Finally, as additional parts of the procure-to-pay function are automated and an electronic audit trail is created, some of the problems will diminish. A lot of the he-said, she-said finger-pointing games will disappear because of the electronic paper trail.

Worst Practice: Worst practices include:

- ✓ Ignoring the customer service implications of the accounts payable function.
- ✓ Not working to share information about accounts payable issues with the rest of the company
- ✓ Not working with purchasing

The Issue: Working with Purchasing

Historically speaking, accounts payable and purchasing have not gotten along in some organizations. This does not have to be. In fact, it is better for both organizations if the two can work harmoniously. As accounts payable has become more integrated into the finance and accounting chain, the sometimes-frayed relationship between the accounts payable and purchasing departments have improved.

What's more, as the accounting function in general, and the accounts payable function and purchasing function specifically, have become more automated providing greater visibility into transactions, the relationship tends to improve.

Some organizations, most notably those <u>not</u> in manufacturing, have taken to merging the two organizations under one manager. By having both functions report to the same manager, some of the frictions have been eliminated.

Best Practice: When establishing policy or trying to work about a problem, try looking at it from the other side of the table. Too often, accounts payable while fully understanding its own issues does not realize the problems purchasing may have. (And of course, the same goes for purchasing sometimes not understanding the issues accounts payable has.).

Looking at the problem from both sides helps both sides work together and craft solutions and procedures that both departments not only can live with but can benefit from.

The old adage of walking a mile in the others shoes is applicable to this situation. Wherever possible, have the purchasing staff spend time working in accounts payable and vice versa. Let the purchasing staff process those invoices that are problematic, let them see all the extra work created by last minute approvals and most of all, let them go through the rigmarole of issuing a Rush check.

Interdepartmental lunches will also help as will monthly (or quarterly) meetings to discuss problems, air out differences, and develop solutions to ongoing problems.

Almost Best Practice: Doing as many of the above as you can but not all.

Special Pointers for Accounts Payable: Accounts payable often has the information that purchasing can use to negotiate better rates. By working with purchasing, accounts payable can give purchasing the information they need to be more successful.

Worst Practice: Letting poor relations with the purchasing department fester.

The Issue: Customer Service in Accounts Payable

Too often when the issue of customer service is mentioned in accounts payable, the first response is "hey we're the customer and we're always right." It is this type of attitude that gets the accounts payable department into hot water with vendors, purchasing and other departments within the organization.

Accounts payable has a variety of customers. They include:

- ✓ Vendors looking for information about payments or invoices
- ✓ Employees looking for information about expense reports
- ✓ Purchasing professionals looking for information for suppliers
- ✓ Other employees looking for information accounts payable may have that will help them with their projects or research
- ✓ Admins looking for information for their bosses

Best Practice: Start by walking a mile in their shoes. Determine the motivation behind their call and what is really driving them. It may not be what your think. For example, an accounts receivable person calling looking for a late payment may not only be looking for the late payment, they may also be concerned about their bonus, if it is linked to how quickly they collect funds.

Similarly, a small business owner calling looking for a late payment may be distressed because he or she needs that money to meet payroll. By understanding the underlying motivation behind the call your staff may be more sympathetic.

Make sure you put an employee with good people skills in the position of answering vendor inquiries and other types of questions. Get to know your employees' strengths and weaknesses. This will help you assign the department's work in a manner that matches each employee's key strengths with the tasks that require those abilities. An employee that is very careful and accurate might be a good person to assign data entry tasks while the gregarious easy-going processor might be the ideal selection to put on the help desk.

Establish a policy of always responding to an inquiry within 24 or 48 hours, even if it is to only tell the person their matter is still being researched. Don't leave them dangling, thinking no one is addressing their issue.

Almost Best Practice: None.

Special Pointers for Accounts Payable: Periodically check and see how the internal customers view the accounts payable department. This means surveying your customers and asking for feedback. It also signals to your customers that their opinions matter. Just the simple act of doing the survey could improve the department's image with the rest of the company. The intelligence that you get from these surveys can be a real eye opener. But getting the information is just the first step. Then you need to take a cold hard look at whatever criticism is given and see if and how the actions that generated the negative feedback can be changed.

Realize that no matter how hard you and your staff try, you will always end up with a few disgruntled customers. Your goal is to try and keep that number to an absolute minimum. Before we close on this issue, there is one more point.

Having a customer service attitude in accounts payable does not mean turning into a doormat, doing whatever anyone asks. You still need to stick to your best practices and strong internal controls. Don't start issuing a Rush check anytime you are asked or returning checks to requisitioners. That might make your customers happy but it is not good for the overall organization. Your goal should be to meet the needs of your customers while maintaining best practices and strong internal controls.

Worst Practice: Worst practices include:

- ✓ Ignoring the customer service aspects of the function
- ✓ Taking a we're-always-right attitude
- ✓ Not looking for ways to meet your customers' needs within the framework of best practices

The Holy Grail: Early Payment Discounts

Chapter 22: Cash Flow Management Issues

Cash flow is the lifeblood of any organization. It is comprised of two flows, cash in and cash out. When it comes to cash flow, accounts payable is all about the cash out. In this chapter we discuss the following issues:

- Taking Early Payment Discounts
- Payment Timing
- Payment Status Information for Vendors

The Issue: Taking Early Payment Discounts

Early payment discounts represent the best investment opportunity any organization has, except perhaps for those in the loan sharking business. Therefore, it is every organization's best interest to identify as many early payment discounts as possible and take them all. One accounts payable manager claims "the only mortal sin in her organization is missing an early payment discount." In a low-interest-rate environment, they are particularly attractive. Of course, as attractive as they are to the customer, they are equally unattractive to the supplier who offers them. So, many suppliers search like crazy to find instances when their customers took early payment discounts but didn't earn them.

Early payment discounts are the concessions vendors sometimes offer their customers in order to entice them to pay early. The most common payment term to incorporate these inducements is 2/10 net 30. It offers customers a 2% discount if they pay the invoice within ten days of receiving the invoice instead of on the 30th day. There are several problems that often arise in connection with the early payment discount.

The first relates to when the clock starts ticking. Usually, the customer and the vendor have a different idea of when the timing starts – the customer believing that the time starts when the invoice hits the accounts payable department while the vendor starts counting on the date on the invoice. Of course, if you receive invoices electronically, this is a non-issue.

Companies sometimes have a difficult time processing invoices in a timely enough manner to qualify for the early payment discount. Let's face it, ten days isn't a lot of time if the invoice has to be:

- ✓ Received in accounts payable
- ✓ Logged in
- ✓ A copy sent to the appropriate person for approval
- ✓ The approver has to review the invoice, approve it and return it to accounts payable
- ✓ The associate in accounts payable has to process the invoice and schedule it for payment
- ✓ The check has to be printed and signed in the appropriate check run, which can be as infrequent as once a week.

Once again, a move to the electronic world solves many of these problems. It also creates an audit trail making it difficult for one party to accuse the other of dragging their feet when in fact; they were the ones who didn't perform as they should.

So, companies sometimes stretch the period and take the discount a few days after the early payment discount period really has ended.

Best Practice: Take all early payment discounts offered. In theory companies should perform an analysis to determine if it is financially advantageous to pay early and take the discount. However, interest rates are so low that such an analysis is a waste of time. When rates are higher, the analysis is an absolute requirement. But it has been a long time since such an analysis was required.

To give you a rough idea, 2/10 net 30 translates to a 36% rate of return. Even a .5/10 net 30 would translate into a 9% rate of return.

Large invoices that involve an early payment discount should be flagged to ensure that they receive priority handling so the discounts are not lost.

Almost Best Practice: None.

Special Pointers for Accounts Payable: Vendors do not appreciate customers who take early payment discounts without paying within the discount period. Some will try and collect the unearned discounts and others will eventually raise prices to cover this charge.

Still others accrue the unearned discounts and when an open credit shows up on the books will use it to clear out the unearned discount accrual.

Some companies stretch the early payment term for a few days and will take the discount say up until the 15th day. Whatever the policy regarding taking discounts after the discount period has ended should be formalized and in writing. Be aware that just because the company has a policy allowing it to take the discount after the discount period has ended, does not mean the vendor will go along with it.

Worst Practice: Worst practices include:

- ✓ Not making taking early payment discounts a priority
- ✓ Taking all discounts even when payments are made after the

discount period and/or after the due date.

The Issue: Payment Timing

Payment timing games are a zero-sum game. For every day the customer gains by paying late, the supplier loses by receiving the payment an equal number of days after the due date. Yet some companies choose to improve their cash flow by stretching their payment dates, usually without the consent of the supplier. Or, if the supplier consents it is because it is an unequal relationship with the customer being the 800-pound gorilla.

While the company stretching the payments may feel they have gained, there are numerous problems associated with this practice. It takes extra work for the payables staff to manage this process, the likelihood that a duplicate payment will be made when the vendor sends a second invoice skyrockets and it hurts vendor relations.

This is not to say that if a company is having cash flow difficulties, it shouldn't stretch payments. Sometimes it has no other choice. But, unless there are cash flow problems, payment stretching creates problems where none existed.

Best Practice: Pay the right vendor, the right amount at the right time. While I wish I had come up with this, it's only fair to give credit where credit is due. This is the mission statement for the accounts payable department at Lowe's Company Inc. Hopefully many others have emulated this policy or developed similar policies.

Almost Best Practice: None.

Special Pointers for Accounts Payable: If your organization insists on stretching payments, especially for more than a few days, pay special attention to your routines for identifying duplicate invoices. For a vendor that is not paid on time will send a second invoice. Rarely are they marked Copy or Duplicate. And occasionally, they will have a different invoice number. This makes it particularly difficult to weed out the duplicates.

If the organization is stretching payments, it is a really good idea to utilize best practices throughout the rest of your accounts payable operation. This will make it a bit easier to identify the duplicates before a second payment is made. And, as those familiar with the duplicate payment issue know only too well, few vendors return a second payment without being prompted by the payee. This can be a costly endeavor involving either staff that could be working on other value-add tasks or hiring a third-party auditor to handle the recoveries. Clearly they don't work for free.

Worst Practice: Worst practices include:

- ✓ Paying early
- ✓ Stretching payments when there is no cash flow issue

The Issue: Payment Status Information for Vendors

One of the problems for accounts payable is the endless phone calls coming into accounts payable from vendors inquiring about the status of their invoices. Most want to know either why they have not been or when they will be paid. Sometimes vendors will call to find out if you've received their invoice and if it has been scheduled for payment.

These calls are disruptive and do not add any value to the payment function. Worse, they require accounts payable to research the particular invoice and return the call. If there were some simple way to share this information with vendors, the number of phone calls coming into accounts payable could be reduced.

While we refer to this issue as payment status, some call it payment visibility.

Best Practice: First, good policies and procedures with regard to the entire invoice handling process will ensure that not only do payments get made in a timely manner but the number of phone calls inquiring about payment status will decline.

Paying on time will also help to reduce the number of calls.

Making this information available on the Internet works very well also. Giving vendors a place to check the information regarding payment and invoice status will make a serious dent in the number of phone calls coming into the department. The information can be put on the Internet. With the appropriate user IDs, passwords and invoice numbers, vendors can check on the status of their invoices and anticipated payments. This functionality is part of some other products being developed for the accounts payable function.

Interactive voice response (IVR) units allow the vendor to call a phone number and in response to several voice prompts get the status of their invoices and the date the check will be cut. This product takes advantage of similar technology to that used by pharmacies that allow you to place orders for prescription refills but did not really take off. This was probably due to the advent of the Internet-based applications. Many invoice automation modules include this feature.

Almost Best Practice: While not the best approach in the world, some companies that have not found a way to institute best practices by trying one or more of the following:

✓ Assign one or more people to the task of answering these calls and researching the invoice status and replying to the vendor with this information.

✓ Limit the time of day when someone in accounts payable will answer vendor inquiries.

✓ Set up an e-mail address where vendors can send inquiries.

✓ Refusing to respond to those vendors who continually call before the payment date to see if the invoice has been received and that there are no problems.

Special Pointers for Accounts Payable: No matter how good the company's payment practices and information sharing facilities, the calls will still come. If the company has implemented some of the best practices and a key vendor calls with an invoice inquiry, someone in accounts payable will have to respond. In order to maintain good vendor relations, it is recommended that every company develop a policy of responding to inquires within 24-48 hours. Once the policy is put in place, make sure the staff adheres to it.

Worst Practice: Worst practices include:

✓ Having whoever answers the phone research the payment or invoice status that the caller has inquired about.
✓ Research and respond to only those invoice inquiries for payments that are more than 30 days past due.

Where's the Paper?

Closing Thoughts

It occurs to me as I finish this work that I've identified a far greater number of worst practices than best practices. And perhaps that is a commentary on best practices. A strategic component in running a best-practice accounts payable operation involves avoiding practices that are likely to cause problems. These difficulties could be as a result of weak controls that enabled fraud or regulatory nightmares or as a result of non-compliance with either state or federal regulations.

But avoiding poor practices is only one part of the equation. Best practices have always been evolving but the speed at which they have been changing in the last few years is truly startling. What this means is that running a best practice operation also means continually evaluating current practices looking for those opportunities to improve while simultaneously identifying those practices which no longer work. Unfortunately, the practices that make an organization leading edge today might not suffice just a few years down the road.

Looking into a crystal ball for the next few years, it is likely that regulatory issues will continue to gain hold as states and the federal government continue to try and close the gaps caused by those not complying. It also is likely that cloud-based innovations will continue to play a significant role in the way the accounts payable function evolves. And evolve it will. Accounts payable is no longer a function operating in its own little silo. It is now an integral part of the accounting and finance chain. And, that is a good thing. And with that, let's take a look at our last issue and last best practice.

The Issue: Preparing for the Future

2020 was a real eye-opener not only for those in accounts payable but for the whole business community. The business world as we knew it got turned over on its head. Things that we never thought possible, became possible. Many organizations took the accounts payable function home on 48 hours' notice. And, much to the surprise of their bosses, they kept their companies running. Not only did they keep them running, but they gained no respect from their bosses.

We learned many things from COVID-19. Perhaps the biggest lesson was that we cannot expect things to continue as they were in the past indefinitely. To expect that our careers and our jobs will continue to function much the same as they did yesterday is an invitation to a very rude awakening.

While we don't know what's coming next, one thing is pretty certain. there will be another upheaval—whether it be another health-related issue such as coronavirus, or a weather-related situation such as a hurricane tornado or perhaps even earthquake we don't know. Of course, I am hoping it won't be terrorist related. The point is that we have to be ready for anything.

Best Practice: Expect the unexpected and be flexible.

Almost Best Practice: None

Special Pointer for Accounts Payable:

Worst Practice: Assuming nothing will change and sticking your head in the sand when it comes to change and new technologies.

Glossary of Terms

ACFE – Association of Certified Fraud Examiners

ACH – Automated Clearing House

ACH credit – An electronic payment initiated by the payor

ACH debit – An electronic payment initiated by the payee

B-Notice - An annual IRS notification to payers, that IRS Forms 1099 have been filed with either missing or incorrect name/TIN combinations.

COVID-19 – see COVID

COVID – worldwide pandemic that forced many businesses to send their employees to work from home

Duplicate Payment – The unintentional second payment of an invoice. One type of erroneous payment and unfortunately, rarely returned by the vendor unless the customer or its audit firm discover the over payment.

e-Invoice – An electronic invoice either provided through an automated approach or as simple attachment to an e-mail. Some do not consider files attached to e-mail as true electronic invoices.

Form 1099 – The Form 1099 is used to report different types of taxable income; the most common for the accounts payable groups being Form 1099MISC. This is used to report income paid to independent contractors.

Internal Controls - The group of policies and procedures implemented within the organization to prevent intentional or unintentional misuse of funds for unauthorized purposes.

MCC - Merchant Category Code

NACHA - National Automated Clearing House Association

NAPCP – National Association of Purchasing Card Professionals

P-card – Sometimes referred to as corporate procurement card or purchasing card.

Packing slip – Sometimes referred to as receiving documents, delineates exactly what was delivered in a particular shipment. Used in the three-way match.

PO – Purchase Order

Receiving documents – See packing slip.

Remote Work – working somewhere other than the company's office

Same Day ACH – an ACH transaction where the funds are available close of business on the day

S-Ox – Sarbanes Oxley Act

Segregation of Duties – With regards to accounts payable, it is the division of work so that one person does not perform more than one leg of the procure-to-pay function. It is one of the foundation principles of strong internal controls.

Three-way Match – Comparison of invoice with purchase order and receiving documents before payment is made. If there is a discrepancy, some investigation is required to eliminate the discrepancy before payment is made.

T&E – Travel and Entertainment

UCC – Uniform Commercial Code

W-2 – Its full name is Wage and Tax Statement. Employers use it to report annual income and tax withholding to the IRS and employees. Typically, there is a copy that goes to the state.

W-9 – Its full name is Request for Taxpayer Identification Number and Certification and it is provided to customers who need to verify certain tax reporting information.

WFH – see working from home

Working from home – performing job at home rather than in company office

RESOURCES

AP Now focuses on producing best practice information needed to run an effective and efficient accounts payable function. It offers both free and fee-based information. Its business intelligence is disseminated in the form of:

- Free ezine
- AP Now podcast
- Accounts payable books
- Memberships
- Newsletter
- Portal of articles
- Twice-a-month webinars

www.ap-now.com

A global organization, headquartered in the UK

- Runs AP Forum, largest AP group on Linkedin
- Membership
- Training, Networking
- Tools, Benchmarking
- Newsletters and Support

https://www.ap-association.com/

Resources Continued

Putting the *AP* **in h***AP***py®**

At Debra R Richardson LLC, we work with Accounts Payable teams to *pay the right vendor,* avoiding fraud and regulatory fines. Check out the website which has free and paid resources for vendor setup and maintenance processes:

- 5 Day Vendor Master File Clean-Up
- Vendor Process ReDesign
- Weekly Blog Posts & Podcast
- AP New & Events / New Scam Alerts
- Free Vendor Process Downloads & Webinars
- Authentication.Validation.Management™ eGuide & Toolkit

www.debrarrichardson.com
www.puttingtheapinhappy.com

Kelly Paxton, CFE, PI
SPEAKER & FRAUD CONSULTANT

THE WORKPLACE
DISHONESTY EXPERT

kellypaxton.com
pinkcollarcrime.com

Resources Continued

Recharged Education serves the Commercial Card/ Purchasing Card community—both industry providers and end-user/buying organizations—by offering:

- **Complimentary educational content related to payment strategies and card program management**
- **Resources available for purchase**
- **Fee-based consulting, training, content development, and more**

www.recharged-education.com

Virtual Tax Attorney

TIR Answer Center subscription includes:

- Expert Answers to Your Questions
- Searchable FAQ
- Tax Tip of the Week & Monthly Articles
- Free and Discounted Webinars

taxinformationreporting.com

ABOUT THE AUTHOR

Mary Schaeffer, AP Now's Founder, was recently named a top 50 Influencer in AP, by the AP Association, a global organization headquartered in the UK. She hosts the weekly AP Now podcast, which can be found on YouTube, iTunes and a variety of other podcasting networks. Her AP influencer status extends to Twitter, where you can find her tweeting using the handle @accountspayable.

Schaeffer has been creating content around the accounts payable function for 20+ years. This material takes the form of a twice-a-week free ezine, a weekly podcast, a monthly newsletter, a variety of courses for accountants, webinars, seminars and the AP Best Practice certificate program.

She has a BS in Mathematics from York College (CUNY) and an MBA in Finance from New York University. Before founding AP Now, she worked in corporate finance and treasury for Continental Grain (Cash Manager) Equitable Life, now AXA (Assistant Treasurer) and O&Y (Financial Risk Manager).

ABOUT THE AP NOW

AP Now is the leading source of accounts payable information for the business and finance community. It offers several different levels of membership, ranging from a simple newsletter membership to a Platinum membership. Corporate (group) memberships are available at significant discounts.

Details can be found at https://www.ap-now.com/

It offers a host of products and services designed to advance your department, your company, and your career. These include:

- ✓ E-AP News weekly ezine (complimentary)
- ✓ The AP Now podcast (complimentary)
- ✓ Accounts Payable Now & Tomorrow Newsletter (monthly fee-based publication delivered by e-mail)
- ✓ Webinars/e-Workshops
- ✓ Seminars
- ✓ Books

Index